Facing A

GW00854481

Roy Ward is a counsellor, accredited by the British Association for Counselling, working in private and NHS general practice. Formerly he was an officer in the Church Army and their Director of Counselling from 1981 to 1991. He has extensive experience in counselling, counselling training and supervision gained over 25 years' practice in London and Manchester.

He lives in Sydenham, South London, with his wife, Elizabeth. They have a grown-up family of a daughter and three sons.

FACING ANXIETY

Roy Ward

TRI△NGLE

First published 1993
Triangle
SPCK
Holy Trinity Church
Marylebone Road
London NW1 4DU

British Library Cataloguing in Publication Data
A catalogue record for this book is available from the British Library.
ISBN 0-281-04673-5

Typeset by Inforum, Rowlands Castle, Hants
Printed in Great Britain by
BPCC Hazell Books
Aylesbury, Bucks
Member of BPCC Ltd

Contents

INTRODUCTION

In over twenty years as a counsellor I have worked with many people who have suffered from anxiety in one form or another and, in what follows, I shall rely heavily on what they have taught me as well as on the wisdom of my various teachers and supervisors. Where I have used examples based on specific individuals, I have only done so with their permission as well as having altered any biographical details to preserve confidentiality.

In addition to my counselling, I have interviewed a number of people specifically for this book and will occasionally use their own words as they describe their experience. Anxiety comes in various forms and is often difficult to express. You may recognise in them feelings of anxiety similar to your own. Perhaps one of the simplest antidotes to anxiety is the knowledge that you are not alone in your distress.

I shall, of course, draw on the experience of anxiety I know best of all, my own.

I shall discuss how anxiety relates to the Christian faith, how faith and the life of the church can be a positive resource for help and, unhelpfully, how religion can be so anxious and defensive itself that it serves to keep the overly anxious person confined and unable to face the inner truth that has the power to liberate.

Finally I shall point the way towards further sources of help for those who are distressed by excessive anxiety and know the misery it can bring.

Roy Ward
March 1993

1
WHAT IS ANXIETY?

Anxiety and Fear

Anxiety is natural to human beings, part of life's rich variety and closely bound up with excitement, energy and creativity – that is, when anxiety is within certain bounds. Too much anxiety limits, constricts and paralyses; in excess it can become a living hell, so intolerable for the sufferer that death may seem to offer the only possible way out. In this first chapter I will give examples which span this range of anxiety from the everyday to the severe.

Anxiety is closely linked to fear. We may be faced by an actual danger to our physical well-being, or even our survival. If, for instance, we encounter a ferocious dog in the park, our response is immediate and sharply focused. Certain bodily changes happen in us quite automatically, equipping us for action, either to face up to the dog or to run away, the 'fight or flight reaction', as it is often called. At the same time our mind too becomes totally preoccupied with the emergency which faces us. Sometimes the sudden reaction may be so intense that we become paralysed by fear but usually we will be able to take appropriate action to deal with the danger. In such a case our feelings of fear subside after a while and our bodily reactions return to a more restful state, though it may take some time for this to happen and we are likely to be more alert and prepared for danger on subsequent visits to the park.

It is important to see that, in physical danger such as this, our instinct for survival works in such a way that we respond automatically and our fear reaction is purely functional, that is, it prepares us to deal with the danger. It is also temporary in that the body and mind return to a state of rest once the danger is past.

A dog may threaten us outwardly; inwardly we also meet threats to our well-being and survival with similar automatic responses which are physical as well as emotional and mental. It could be said that *fear* relates to threats to our physical or material survival while *anxiety* relates to the danger we feel to our inner self, our soul and mind. Attempts to separate fear and

1

anxiety in this way are useful to some extent, but to push the distinction too far would be to ignore the complexity of our human responses and over-simplify the reality of people's experience. Words can also be used to suggest the different tone and intensity of feelings. In what follows I will tend to use 'anxiety' to refer to our response to threats to the inner self, the soul or mind; however, 'fear' and 'anxiety' will not be strictly separated and certainly those people I quote use the words as seems best to them, and others as well, such as apprehension, nervousness, dread, terror and panic. Each word gives a different shade and tone of the primary colour of *fear*.

Here is an example where threats to the body and threats to the inner self are interwoven, an incident involving a middle-aged man, an Anglican vicar, on the local golf-course.

> John is an inexperienced golfer who has taken up the game partly, it would seem, to go along with his teenage son, Stephen, who is learning to play. The incident was triggered by as small a crime as cutting ahead of someone on the tee. John reported:
>
>> This guy threatened to beat me up with his club, which I found pretty traumatic. I tried to be calm but he wasn't listening, he was swearing at me. Stephen was with me and I was concerned about him . . . on two levels: I didn't want to get into a fight and secondly I didn't want to seem a wimp to Stephen. There was that anxiety and anyway, how do you face a totally irrational person? I actually had to go home, I couldn't stay at the golf-course.

The vicar experiences what is a very understandable feeling of fear when faced with the prospect of a fight. His fear is intensified by the irrational nature of the attack on him because he cannot reason with the other man and he is on very unfamiliar ground as, like most vicars, he is not used to fist-fighting. At the same time, even in the middle of such an emergency, he is anxious about how he will appear in the eyes of his son. Will he seem a wimp and be discredited as a father if he runs away or will he continue to be admired and respected by his son?

The problem goes even deeper than what his son will think of him: John projects a part of himself on to his son, that is, he sees himself as if through Stephen's eyes, and is in danger of losing respect for himself, even despising himself, if he loses face. After all, John grew up like most boys of his generation thinking that to be a proper man meant to be brave and fearless. Although his Christian faith has gone some way to helping him accept himself as he really is, that is as God knows him, fears included, there remain those hidden self-doubts, known to most of us, about not being good enough, which can be so powerfully brought to the surface by unexpected events. So John's anxiety is more to do with the danger he feels to his view of himself as a person and his value as a man than to anything else though it is intimately linked to the physical fear of having his head beaten by a golf-club.

Children may chant at each other, 'Sticks and stones may break my bones but names will never hurt me', but this is said more with bravado than inner conviction and truth. Though there are those who are profoundly secure in their sense of self-hood and those whose psychological defences are pretty impregnable, the majority of us are vulnerable to attacks and threats to our inner being and are consequently prone to anxiety when danger looms or, more precisely, when danger is believed to threaten.

The Body's Response to Fear

When we are afraid, what we experience at a physical level is the body preparing itself to respond to an emergency by means of fight or flight. Some animals are best adapted to one response, some to the other, though all the higher animals are capable of both. The reactions occur quite automatically by a series of re-flexes involving the nervous system in a way that is outside our conscious control. These changes are such that energy is increased in the muscles of the limbs, the heart beats faster, breathing is deeper and more rapid, the pupils dilate to improve vision and generally the body is more alert. At the same time changes take place in the digestive system as the bladder and bowels empty and the system closes down. Thus the body is keyed up for action.

These reactions are purely functional for an animal living in the wild or for human beings in a primitive environment and, of course, they happen in moments of danger to us all. The sensation of fear associated with these physical changes is an unpleasant one and, as with pain, it spurs us to do something about it, to overcome any inertia and, through some appropriate action, make ourselves safe. Once the emergency is past we will tend to return to a relaxed state in which the physical processes described above revert to normal though, perhaps, not completely so. Particularly if we are encountering a danger for the first time or if it is a situation of high risk we may take a long while to unwind and feel apprehensive whenever we approach similar situations in the future. I am reminded of my beagle puppy when she was a few months old. Her walks in the park were joyful and carefree events in which she considered everyone, human and canine, as her friends. One day a German Shepherd dog, who she thought was good for a game, picked her up by the scruff of the neck and shook her violently before throwing her to the ground. She ran in terror. After that and for the rest of her life she displayed fear by the raising of hair along her spine whenever we entered the park, and the appearance of a German Shepherd was the signal for the twin emotions of fear and aggression.

For many of us living in twentieth-century Britain, especially adults with sedentary jobs, our most common experience of serious physical danger is driving, particularly on the motorways. Although we may not consciously feel afraid, we operate at a level of alertness which is essential for our survival and that of other road-users in this potentially deadly situation. Our fearful alertness is translated into action through our control and mastery of the vehicle as we overcome (or overtake) the hazards around us. This fear of what is indeed real danger is lessened by the illusion of safety provided by modern cars: comfortable seats, a smooth ride, noise reduction and music. If, however, we pass an accident we tend to drive with increased care and attention, at least for a few minutes. If the accident happens to us, the fear digs so deep into us that it may shake our normal self-confidence for a long while, in some cases so that we never drive again.

4

Symptoms of Anxiety

The symptoms of anxiety are varied and complex, so to try to make them clearer I will look at three categories: physical, psychic (of the mind or soul) and behavioural.

From a physical point of view the symptoms of anxiety are essentially the same as those of fear. There are automatic changes in the body, over which we have no direct control, which are designed to prepare for action when a threat is in sight.

A typical example is given by Trevor, an ordained minister with fifteen years' experience. He is normally energetic, sociable and confident and thought of as a strong leader by his congregation. He spoke to me about feeling anxious when he has to preach:

It's my stomach, my guts which are affected. This is where I get it most potently. If I am very anxious my stomach tightens, feels uncomfortable. If it's an acute attack I get diarrhoea, my heart will beat faster as well, but it affects my guts before anything else. I can only really describe it as a knotting up, a tenseness in the abdomen but much deeper than that, within the bowel. And you become aware you have bits in there you normally take for granted, then suddenly you're aware they're there. It's terribly difficult to put into words but, if you want me to localise it, that's where it is.

That's the initial feeling I get to the extent that, if I've got a service or am entering a confrontation situation, then I will feel this tightness, this knotting. I will find I'm going to the loo several times. My bowels just generate more and more excrement. It's very potent.

This sort of stomach upset is familiar to many people though the person suffering from it may find, like Trevor, that they cannot get across to other people the full force of it or how distressing it feels to be in the grip of such a powerful reaction to threat. Some physical symptoms are even more difficult to describe, like that of Clare.

Clare describes herself as 'a stressed type of person' and says that she becomes anxious about almost every area of her life. I asked Clare how she feels when she suffers a moderately bad attack of anxiety.

> Well, I suppose it starts just under the rib-cage and works its way up to a prickly sensation in my scalp. I suppose I'm slightly breathless, not as bad as a panic attack. I feel this welling up from just under the rib-cage going right up to the top of my scalp. It's like a wave.

I asked her what the wave was. Was it pain? She went on,

> No! It's a sensation, an unpleasant sensation. It can fluctuate throughout whatever is occurring, that's causing me to feel anxious. Or, if I've gone to sleep and forgotten it, I can wake up in the morning and without actually putting it into words in my mind, the sensation is there before the thought.

This sensation appears to be the only physical symptom Clare notices, apart from the slight breathlessness. Even this symptom is hard for her to describe and is elusive with its comings and goings. To the casual observer Clare's experience of an unpleasant sensation might seem trivial and not very disturbing, but it is clear listening to her tone of voice that it causes her considerable stress.

This is true for many people who suffer anxiety. For some the physical symptoms of anxiety are more obvious. If the stress and anxiety of an attack go on persistently, and the person does not relax, it may result in a variety of physical conditions which are brought on or made worse by a threatening situation.

Jim, a young man and a Christian, described to me such symptoms:

> There are physical symptoms when I'm anxious. My psoriasis [the skin complaint] gets bad. I say, 'What am I worried about?' I get severe headaches and have to go to bed for 24 hours.
>
> For four or five years I had a urinary complaint. I had to

go to the lavatory four or fives times a night. The doctor couldn't find anything. I felt it was stress related. You become anxious about the symptoms.

Jim recognises these symptoms of his as signals of anxiety, although he does not necessarily feel worried at the time. He came to me because he wanted to work out what he really is worried about. People are often referred for counselling in this kind of condition. They say that their doctor thinks that the symptoms they have reported are evidence of anxiety and stress, although the patient has no idea they are worried or anxious about anything. Sent to a counsellor, they often turn up very doubtful about the need for counselling and quite resistant to opening up about themselves. They feel that the counsellor's interest in things like their family relations and work situation can have little or no relevance to their physical illness. Some people like that do take the opportunity to look behind the wall they have erected; others choose not to explore what is going on, others seem so out of touch with their feelings that they are more unable than unwilling to use the opportunity.

The time was when many doctors seemed not to recognise the effect of anxiety and other emotional conditions on the physical health of patients. Now there seems to be much greater understanding though, I have to say, we must be careful in case the stress and anxiety become too convenient as explanations.

In our civilised world anxiety may be the reaction to a situation in which physical fight or flight is inappropriate; we therefore try to ignore or control the urgent demands of our bodies for action but, in doing this, we create an internal conflict. The attempt to deny or suppress fear produces further physical symptoms which we associate with anxiety. Some of these I have already mentioned; others include trembling, sweating, palpitations, dry mouth and muscular pains, as well as odd sensations. I want to describe a situation now in which this conflict between the need for fight or flight and the person's effort at self-control might happen.

Jill, a young woman, goes for a job interview. She wants to create a good impression, seem quiet, efficient and self-contained, but the very situation of being interviewed by a panel of people makes her anxious. Her body reacts automatically because she feels threatened and it goes into action: her heart rate increases and her breathing deepens, she wants the lavatory (although she has been careful not to drink for the past two hours), her limbs become ready for moving energetically and her whole body is keyed up. The physical changes make her feel uncomfortable but she controls herself to meet the demands of the situation and to think clearly about the questions she is being asked.

There is now a conflict between her bodily desire to act energetically and her determination to be calm and to smile serenely at her interviewers to assure them of a confidence she does not feel. Her increasing rate of respiration is by now making her sweat uncomfortably and her knuckles are white as she grips them to prevent her hands shaking. She is becoming more and more aware of her anxiety and less and less able to concentrate thoughtfully on answering the questions. She has become, in short, anxious about being anxious. Completely unaware of her own action, she gets hold of a strand of hair and curls it round and round her finger in the very way she used to when she was a little girl trying to get to sleep.

Because she has been breathing too quickly she has hyperventilated just enough to make her feel dizzy so that, when she finally stands up to leave at the end of the interview, the floor feels spongy and she feels slightly odd, slightly out of touch with reality. By the time she gets home, to round off a bad day Jill has a tension headache.

Of course there are dozens of variations on this scene and by no means all the situations develop badly or so alarmingly but it shows the basic conflict between the automatic reactions of the body and the person's conscious wish for self-control. We see, too, some evidence of the mental or psychic symptoms which accompany anxiety. In the case of Jill it begins quite mildly with uneasiness about being interviewed and escalates towards an urgent desire to get away from the room. She loses any clarity of thought and cannot concentrate on the questions she is being asked. By the time she leaves, she has a distinct feeling of unreality which is itself so distressing that it tends to make her even more anxious as she feels less and less in control. This is further accentuated by the spongy feel to the floor as she leaves.

Feelings of unreality like those experienced here are among the most distressing mental symptoms of anxiety, all the more so as the sufferer finds them even harder to explain satisfactorily than the physical symptoms already mentioned. People may say they feel such unreality as being like a dream or nightmare and they frequently feel they are going mad. Such anxiety may cause a deepening terror and fear of impending death or some other unnamed and indefinable fate.

In the case of the young woman I have just described, physical and mental symptoms appear together; this is common, but not inevitable. Mental symptoms and strange sensations may occur separately.

One man, again in an interview situation, described himself as split into two, as if one self was somewhere in the corner of the room, up by the ceiling, looking down on the other self being interviewed by the selection board. He said he felt no sensation of fear and was not consciously anxious at the time though later, once the interview was over and he had got away, he realised how anxious he had been about an interview that was so important for his future.

It can be a considerable relief to people to recognise that some strange mental experience, which they secretly fear as growing insanity, is a form of anxiety.

The third category of symptoms, the behavioural ones, are not greatly in evidence in the case of Jill, the interviewee, though they are certainly present. Her hands give away some of her discomfort. At first, you may assume, she attempts to keep them relaxed in her lap but soon she begins to clench them in a growing effort to control them and hold herself still even though it is a fearful situation. Despite this effort, her general tenseness and her body's desire for flight leaks out, as it were, in the action of curling her hair more and more tightly round her finger in the way she has always used to comfort herself.

Such actions are numerous and psychologists call them

9

'displacement activities'. They may be minute gestures like patting your hair, licking your lips or straightening your dress or tie, or they may be more persistent actions like drumming your fingers or tapping your foot. Nail-biting, smoking, eating, fidgeting – the list is endless, all betraying the inner conflict between the urgent need for action and the need to stay calm and controlled.

To people around who notice these gestures in someone else, it may be perfectly obvious that the restless behaviour of that person shows how anxious they are though they may not suffer, consciously, from any of the physical or mental symptoms I have spoken about. Therefore, were you to ask if the person felt nervous, they might say 'No!' with perfect frankness.

> Clare, whom I have already mentioned, told me about a number of symptoms which she clearly recognises as signs of anxiety in herself. These are all changes to her behaviour.

> > I do drink a lot of tea, a great deal of tea, and I suppose initially if a situation presented itself to me right this moment to make me incredibly anxious I'd go completely off my food for a very short time and then hit the chocolate. And that's a comfort.

> As we went on, Clare became agitated, not surprisingly, by the business of thinking over and talking about anxiety, and she noticed that she had begun to twist her wedding ring round her finger. She said:

> > I tend to hold on to something when I'm anxious; it's usually a bunch of keys. I don't play with the keys but I feel them in the palm of my hand. That's significant. It's security again, isn't it? Even if I'm walking round the shops, I don't put them in my pocket, I hold them like that.

It seems that such behavioural symptoms, as I have called them, are not merely haphazard activities, random ways of getting rid of nervous energy, but actions which have some sort of meaning for the individual. Clare, for example, comments that her holding on to the keys is a sign of her need for security. Similarly she notices how her eating and drinking habits, when she is anxious, give her a feeling of comfort. This may be because eating and drinking remind her, unconsciously, of the comfort and security she first experienced as a baby feeding in her mother's arms. You will notice that people often turn to some kind of gesture or behaviour to do with the mouth when they are anxious. Several have been mentioned already. This is not surprising, given that the earliest way of relating we experience, once outside the womb, is through our mouths sucking at our mother's breast (or whatever substitutes for it). If this is a good experience it becomes a very basic experience of security which later we can recall when we are feeling less secure. It is, perhaps, also unsurprising in the light of this that Jesus chose eating and drinking as the central act of worship, in the holy communion, symbolising the relationship between God and the church.

2
SOME EFFECTS
OF ANXIETY

Family Relationships

When we are anxious it has all kinds of effects on our relationships with other people. Our feelings are disturbed, and we are so preoccupied with whatever is causing the anxiety that we have less than usual time and energy to give to the people around us. As a result, we may withdraw from emotional relationships and into ourselves; or, on the other hand, we may want to get very close to people and avoid being alone. We may find ourselves clinging to our loved ones in a rather desperate way.

To make matters even more complicated, we may want a mixture of these two so that other people who are normally close to us do not know how to do the right thing for us; they are either too close or not close enough. This mixture was described to me by Ben, a social worker, in his interview:

> I have a general feeling of tension, a growing obsession with these feelings so they take up more and more of my thinking time and begin to exclude other things, effectively forcing me into inactivity, preoccupied with the object of the anxiety. If I am really anxious I become less communicative with people and irritable. I absent myself from the family; cease to talk to them. Sometimes I cancel journeys away from home.

In our conversation it became increasingly obvious that his difficulties in relating to his family caused him most concern. He cannot tolerate being close to them because he does not have the psychological space to cope with normal family demands and has to withdraw from them. At the same time he cannot bear to be separated from them as they are such a source of security and love for him. At such times he makes a compromise by being in the same house as the family, within sight and sound of them, but not actually involved in all the activity and emotional rough and tumble of family life. There is probably a fine line for the family to tread between ignoring him so that he feels isolated, and irritating him with their demands.

The Effect of Anxiety on Sexual Relations

Even for people comfortable with their sexuality and with a generally satisfying sex life, a spell of unusual anxiety can have an immediate impact on sexual feelings and performance. This is, perhaps, more obvious in a man than a woman in that the man's erection may be the first thing to suffer when he is anxious but, of course, both sexes are affected. The man may fail to get an erection at all or get one but lose it at the moment of penetration. If he can take this as being a passing nuisance, due to stress or tiredness, which will soon put itself right, all well and good, but if he becomes anxious about this new problem, in addition to whatever anxiety he is already feeling, it can create a vicious circle. The matter is made worse by the fact that his whole sense of manhood may be strongly tied up to his sexual potency and, as a man cannot have an erection by a direct act of will, he feels extremely vulnerable and even more anxious than before.

Malcolm became impotent for a time when his small business began to go downhill. As well as being anxious and preoccupied about the survival of his business, he was physically tired as a result of long hours at work. When he tried to make love he was not aroused in his usual way and felt he had let his wife down. So the next night, although he was tired, he was both determined to try again and over-anxious to perform well. Not surprisingly, he failed. He got only a partial erection and even that failed at the vital moment. Because he was already feeling something of a failure over the business and worried that he would not be able to provide for the family, this sexual failure added considerably to his sense of inadequacy and he became quite depressed.

The more he tried the more impotent he became. Next he attempted to avoid his growing anxiety about the situation by withdrawing altogether from any sexual relations with his wife. And she, who unfortunately had no understanding of his anxiety, responded by becoming irritated as her own sexual

13

frustration grew. This developed into mutual criticism and a number of rows about other issues.

At this stage they decided to ask for some professional help and, as their relationship was basically very good, they were able to work together at their problems in a more creative way.

You can see in this example how easily anxiety in one area builds up anxiety in another and, especially, how anxiety about your sexual performance can be self-defeating. An important part of the counselling for Malcolm and his wife was to encourage them to stop trying to have intercourse for a period of time. This was a great relief for them both and his wife was able to explain that her irritation had less to do with her sexual frustration and more to do with her anxiety that Malcolm's partial impotence was a sign of something deeply wrong with the relationship.

Some women mask the effects of anxiety on their sexual behaviour rather more successfully than men can do by faking their sexual response, though the truth can be that all sexual desire in them has shut down and that, despite their best efforts and those of their partner, they cannot feel a spark of excitement, let alone the fuller satisfaction of an orgasm. In fact they may feel the very opposite of desire: an active dislike, even a sense of revulsion, at the whole sexual performance. If a woman already feels insecure in the relationship with her partner or fears he will take her unresponsiveness as an attack on his manhood, she may try to hide it. Similarly, if she is anxious that she is less of a woman because she is not responding sexually, she may fake it, fearing the accusation, you could say the condemnation, that she is frigid.

Despite much freer attitudes to sex in the second half of this century, it is still an area of life infected by fear and anxiety and for some people the effects are chronic. This may mean that impotence, a lack of sexual response and other such things are not temporary problems such as I have just described but much longer term problems. These may drive virtually all sexual feelings underground or result in some kind of limitation or distortion to a full and satisfying sexuality. Such difficulties can have their roots in childhood experiences which happen long before some adults think of the child as having any sexual awareness at all. They may have to do with the parents' confused and repressive attitudes to anything sexual; or with the complex feelings of love, fear and jealousy between mother, father and child; or with more obvious sexual events and traumas, sometimes with incidents of actual sexual abuse.

For some people the degree of openness and self-abandonment involved in sexual intimacy arouses far too much anxiety for it to be endured, let alone enjoyed. They may feel their strong sexual desires are not decent or that their bodies are not nice or that if they let themselves go they would be consumed by their lustful desires and become promiscuous. They may avoid sexual relationships altogether or limit their behaviour in love-making to a set of strict rituals which protects them from the risk of being too spontaneous. In practice this means that their love-making always follows a set procedure with each familiar step as predictable as the steps in a square dance. The thought of going outside this routine results in immediate anxiety, so any change is carefully avoided. The danger is that they, to say nothing of their partner, may sooner or later find their sex life so sterile and unsatisfactory that it causes a real crisis in the relationship which they then have to face.

While some people are put off sex when they feel anxious and others find their performance is adversely affected, yet others feel an increased desire and look for sexual experiences of one sort or another as a antidote to anxiety. As a counsellor I am not sure of the extent to which this happens under the pressure of anxiety in stable sexual relationships but it is noticeable in other areas of activity. People who are particularly tempted to illicit sexual behaviour of some kind can find themselves much more powerfully drawn to it during periods of unusual anxiety. Of course, their anxiety may be further inflamed by this heightened desire and they may well need skilled professional help to work out their problems.

Anxiety and Excitement: A Positive Note

This book attends mostly to the more disturbing and destructive aspects of anxiety, but it will be helpful to stop for a moment and note the more positive side, mentioned at the start of the book. Fear and anxiety can quite fairly be called forms of excitement: excitement that gears us up to deal with situations which demand a lot of energy. If you doubt the close relationship of fear and excitement then remember what happens on the rides at the fairground which rely heavily on transforming one into the other.

We have seen how anxiety can get out of hand and become destructive and disabling as in the case of Jill's interview. But in a milder form the anxiety, if it had not escalated in the way it did, could have sharpened Jill up emotionally and mentally to give a good performance. You may have noticed that even when your anxiety level is quite high in anticipation of a threatening situation, like taking an exam or having to do something in front of other people, once you can actually get to grips with the task in hand, the anxiety has a way of transforming itself into excitement and energy which is creative and helps you to turn in a good performance. Indeed, some people use anxiety quite deliberately to vitalise their performance.

> Trevor, whom I mentioned earlier, said how he felt when preparing to preach. It is something he has done literally hundreds of times in his ministry as week after week he has prepared for the Sunday service and has felt the stomach-churning symptoms of anxiety he has already described. But then, he says,

>> Once I get into the building (the church) there is a calmness which comes over me. The anxiety becomes something which is creative and positive, exciting. Your mind is working fast, engaged. You're thinking on your feet. I can only describe it as going into a higher gear.

Trevor does not consciously choose to make himself anxious to obtain a better performance, though he does recognise his anxiety as part of the cost of what he does. However, some people do choose this. One woman who works in West End theatre told me that in a long-running show there is always the danger that repetition night after night will lead to a flat, lifeless performance. So members of the cast will sometimes play tricks on each other on the stage and in the middle of a performance to create a level of anxiety and vitality for the sake of themselves and the audience.

An amateur drama group at work gives an example of the progress of anxiety. In this case there is no need to stimulate anxiety as it arises quite spontaneously in the course of the rehearsals and, hopefully, is converted into excitement at the time of the performance. At the early rehearsals there is no anxiety as people chat and joke, but by three weeks before the first performance, with sixty per cent of the cast still dependent upon their scripts, there is a rising anxiety accompanied by a rising level of irritability. In the last week anxiety has turned into imminent panic, rage or despair according to individual temperament. Two people are still attached to their scripts like Linus to his blanket. People vow never to take part in one of the group's productions again. An anxious desire for flight is obviously about as some of the cast consider cancelling the performance even at this late date.

The effect of all this anxiety is to concentrate the mind and will on the task in hand and, come the performance, it begins to transform into excitement and vitality as the catalyst of the audience works its magic. By the final curtain people are on a high and, all anxiety forgotten, are planning the next production.

The transformation of anxiety into excitement, positive energy and creativity seems most frequently to happen when the moment of actually being able to get to grips with the situation has arrived, as in the case of Trevor's preaching or the amateur drama group. Though, as we have already noted in the example of Jill's job interview, this may not happen but instead may increase the anxiety to a disabling degree. Fritz Perls, the founder of Gestalt therapy, called anxiety 'the gap between now and then'. By this he meant that when we are fully engaged in the present moment we do not feel anxious. However, we must remember that to be fully engaged means to be free from the inhibiting effects of defensiveness, such as we shall consider later on.

Anxiety and Aggression

In the case of the amateur drama group, as elsewhere, we find anxiety is closely linked to aggression, irritability, anger and rage. This is hardly surprising when we consider that the flight reaction, running away in fear, is intimately linked to the fight reaction, hitting out at what is threatening. It seems that some people characteristically respond fearfully whilst others respond aggressively. Traditionally, in our culture, society has tended to accept fear and anxiety as fitting the female role whilst aggression in women has been frowned on. At the same time aggression in men has been praised whilst fear and anxiety have brought shame and derision. Largely as a result of the women's movement and the assertive energy that has arisen from their sense of injustice, this gap between the sexes over anxiety and aggression has somewhat narrowed in recent years; women are able to feel and show more aggression and men to feel and show greater fear and anxiety and other such 'weak' emotions as grief without so much disabling shame. At least a change has begun though, I fear, such far reaching change as this, at basic levels of our identity, inevitably meets with powerful resistance in us and takes generations to accomplish thoroughly.

Anxiety and anger are also linked in this way as each may cause the other to increase in an upward spiral. That is to say that if someone makes you feel the pain and discomfort of anxiety, it may cause you to feel angry that they have threatened you. However, if this angry response is towards a person who has power over you or on whom you are dependent, you may become anxious that you will lose control and voice your anger in a way that will reflect badly on you and do you harm.

Michael, a man in middle management, had a new senior manager appointed over him. He feared, with little real cause, that the new man would want him out and what he believed to be this threat to his position in the firm made him very anxious. Immediately his anxiety was followed by anger that the senior manager had the power to threaten him in this way. He felt this anger so intensely that he feared that in their meetings he would easily give way to it and so increase the likelihood of being removed. This heightened anxiety in turn gave way to anger of an almost murderous intensity and, of course, his fear that this would erupt like a volcano drove his anxiety to an even higher pitch.

A similar dilemma was experienced by Margaret, a young woman still living at home with her parents long after she needed, for her own sake and probably for theirs, to move away. When she was going out anywhere on her own she felt a strong pressure to tell her parents where she was going but if she obeyed this inner voice her evening was spoilt because she felt resentful and angry that she still 'had' to tell them like a child. If on the other hand she resisted the urge, her evening was spoilt by feeling anxious and guilty that she had rebelled. She was in an emotional trap from which she could find no escape.

In both these cases it is not the immediate situation which is the problem but the emotionally confused and conflicting inner world the individual brings to bear on the current situation. Anxiety and anger which have their roots in the past distort and magnify feelings caused by present-day events and relationships.

Acute Anxiety and Panic

There is a distinction made by some experts between what they call 'primary' anxiety and 'signal' anxiety. The former is a deep and fundamental fear of primitive intensity about the death or dis-integration of the self. The latter is a warning anxiety which tells us that some situation in which we find ourselves and which stirs up our inner feelings threatens to expose us to the more dreadful fear of primary anxiety. For the most part the signal anxiety works pretty well so that we are not caused to suffer the intensity of primary anxiety. The only glimpse some people get into the terrors of such anxiety may come in occasional nightmares but for those who experience full-blown anxiety states, it can be as if their sleeping nightmares had taken over their waking day.

The examples of anxiety we have considered so far do not illustrate the intensity of primary anxiety though Ben, the social worker, did go on to describe feelings which are on the edge of such a condition as he senses the awfulness of what lies beyond. Journeys even in the company of his family are sometimes im-possible, as if to go away from familiar ground is to risk great danger.

> Sometimes I cancel journeys. I feel a nameless fear of going away, a fear that to go away will make things worse. I feel a fear of upsetting the balance, fear of impending doom, things falling apart.

This sense of 'a nameless fear' and 'impending doom' which appears in more extreme forms of anxiety with almost over-whelming force is particularly difficult for sufferers to convey to family, friends and helpers, who have not themselves experienced the strength of such irrational anxiety. Carers may want the feelings to be described in more concrete terms to which they can more easily relate, like 'I'm afraid of dying'. But the sufferer is not only concerned with the well-being of the body but of the inner self. ('And do not fear those who kill the body but cannot kill the soul' (Matthew 10.28).) The expression of powerful dread which cannot be explained but which threatens to over-whelm the anxious person arouses deep uneasiness in the carer to the extent that he or she may wish to push it down or explain it away for their own comfort.

In Ben's case his level of anxiety is disturbing as he senses the closeness of some disaster to his spiritual and psychological being even though he does not experience the full force of prim-ary anxiety. He is able to follow the warnings of his signal anxiety by staying safe and keeping his family close at hand. This limits his freedom to some extent and, if it happened often, it could become quite disabling. As it is, his experience of it is infrequent though, like much anxiety, it is unpredictable; it may happen under certain circumstances on one occasion but not on another in what appear to be identical circumstances.

The unpredictability of anxiety attacks is an added burden for those who suffer them in this way. Even when they are feeling confident and in good form they are constantly on the watch, in a state of readiness for an attack to strike. They are like people living on thin ice who have already experienced disastrous mo-ments when the ice has split under them and plunged them into the dark waters beneath. This theme of unpredictability is taken up by Betty in describing what happened to her.

Betty is a young teacher and a member of the parish church

where she often reads the lessons at the family service. People who do not know her very well think of her as confident and humorous. They do not suspect the intensity of the anxiety attacks from which she suffers. She manages to keep up a good front even while all hell has broken loose inside her. She says of an acute anxiety attack:

> It's like a wave breaking over you. This wave hits you and then, maybe as the water starts to drip off a bit, you can start fighting it and win over it. But there is a point where it's so intense that you feel you can't do anything. The first time it happened I was reading the Gospel and it just hit me like a wave and it had never happened before and I was totally . . . you know, I was so much afraid of it happening again, I couldn't face that horrible feeling again . . . I climbed into the pulpit and it hit me before the end of the first verse, then I just read to the end of the page, not presenting it, not delivering it, just reading it, and then I turned over the page and it went suddenly, just went, and I was OK till at the end it came back.
> RW So there's an unpredictable quality?
> Yes! That's what's so frightening about it. I think I can just deal with it, then it goes away altogether or might come back. Or it might not happen at the beginning, it might hit me half way through. I could be anywhere doing anything. I feel I don't want to live through that again, I must stop that from happening.

The person who suffers a full-blown anxiety attack, who is subject to the full force of primary anxiety, has gone beyond the limits of their normal emotional experience. Psychologically it may be said that their defences have failed, poetically that they have fallen into the abyss of dread.

I asked Betty what she would say to people listening to her describing her feelings who might think that the pain suffered in the dentist's chair was at least as bad as anything she might feel reading the lesson in church. She said,

> I think it's the worst sort of fear, a terrible fear that I'm going to pieces. It's like there's something horrible out

there that's out to get me and I'm going to dissolve. It's absolute fear. I look around the congregation and they are quite friendly people who smile and I think, 'What on earth am I afraid of?' But when it hits me they change into lions or something. Everything takes on a sinister aspect, so the normal sort of things suddenly seem very threatening.

I fear being out of control, people seeing me out of control like at any minute I'm going to start screaming the place down or running like a loony out of the back doors.

When Betty looks around the congregation and sees the familiar, normally friendly faces, she knows rationally that there is nothing to cause her anxiety. But knowing this makes no difference in the face of the overwhelming anxiety that washes over her. What she knows in her head cannot stem the tide of anxiety though it may prove an important anchor to external reality so that she may fear madness but not give way to it. Would-be helpers often point out to the sufferer of anxiety attacks that 'There is nothing to be afraid of' as if to do so could at once solve the problem. People are often surprised when clearly intelligent people suffer anxiety and other forms of psychological distress as if intelligence were by itself an insurance against such disturbance. They imply that emotional and mental suffering is a manifestation of stupidity.

In practice, if you suffer acute anxiety you may feel a total split between thinking, which remains accurately aware of external reality, and images and sensations which are of another quality altogether. When Betty talks about the people changing into lions, she does not mean that literally and does not think it even in the midst of her most distressing anxiety. Were she to do so she would have crossed over into the realm of psychosis where metaphors lose their 'as if' quality. In her case she knows throughout that the people are people but that fact does not greatly alter her disturbing and psychologically chaotic response.

Betty's phrase 'absolute fear' is particularly striking. It has echoes of the words in the first letter of St John (4.18) that 'perfect love casts out fear.' If that is so, the experience of acute anxiety is that perfect, that is to say, absolute fear casts out love and indeed, faith and hope. In such absolute fear death may seem the only possible escape. The last person I want to talk about in this chapter was driven to a point of desperation where he did consider death as the only way out.

Graham is a 46-year-old engineer, married with two sons. He is deeply committed to the Christian faith and has been since he was a teenager. When he was in his mid-thirties he had an anxiety attack of such intensity that it brought him to the edge of suicide and markedly changed his personality. His life had been very full between work, family and the church, each putting rather more pressure on him than he could sensibly sustain.

When he was thirteen his father had died very suddenly and, although Graham had carried on as if nothing of major significance had occurred, it had shattered his inner world. When the elder of his two sons reached thirteen Graham experienced a sudden and quite unexpected feeling of inadequacy about his role as a father and from then on began to suffer from disturbing feelings of unreality from time to time. He said that he felt at times that he was in a dream (although he knew clearly enough that he was awake and what was happening), and that this state disturbed him profoundly. It only happened when he was away from home and disappeared as soon as he returned; the anxiety was strong enough to make him want desperately to run away but he was able to hold on and somehow contain the feeling.

Graham avoided a few of the situations which most gave rise to these strange feelings, like big crowds, but generally carried on much as before until, after almost a year, he was away overnight on a business trip some two hundred miles from home. He awoke feeling his dream state very strongly and with it the urge to run home. This feeling gave way to an intense and overwhelming feeling of dread. The physical symptoms were of sweating and trembling and he sensed what he later described as 'waves of fear, like a current, going through my body'. He said, 'I felt I couldn't survive, not that I would actually die, but like I would fall apart. I didn't know how I could go on.'

After an hour or so the symptoms had abated but he

continued to sweat and to experience waves of dreadful anxiety every few minutes. He expected everything to return to normal upon arriving home after a nightmare journey but they simply continued in the same pattern for the next two weeks.

During this period he was unable to leave the house and in his worst moments found that even moving from room to room caused a rise in anxiety for which he had to grit his emotional teeth. He was offered sympathetic understanding by his wife and by the vicar but felt that, despite all their efforts to understand, he was unable to put into meaningful words his inner anguish. He prayed often but felt that God was remote and that perhaps his suffering was a form of divine punishment. This idea went against every belief he held but remained an insistent, half-unconscious fear. Most of all Graham feared that there was no escape from the torment of his anxiety state and that his fate was sealed in it.

In the following months he experienced repetitions of the original, intense anxiety state and each time was plunged into weeks of after-shock. His doctor urged him to take tranquillisers but he feared that if he took them they might cause great mental confusion which would make his condition worse. He equally dreaded the possibility of a psychiatric hospital and a descent into madness. Thoughts of suicide began to come into Graham's mind. Death presented itself as the only remaining way out of the seemingly intolerable physical, mental and spiritual distress.

He said that there were three compelling factors which he was able to set against the suicidal impulse. The first of these was that to die prematurely would be to cause his children to suffer a distress similar to that which he himself had suffered as a young person by the death of his father. His love for them would not allow that. The second was that he feared that to die in such a state of anxiety might fix him eternally in an emotional and spiritual hell. He said by way of illustration, 'My mum used to say "Don't pull a face like that; if the wind changes you'll get stuck" '. Third, he retained a small measure of faith in God, what he called 'a pinhead of faith', which he did not feel in an emotional sense, nor could argue in an intellectual way. But he felt that in his most distressing state that was all that really remained.

Graham did not commit suicide, though sometimes people are driven to that extreme by the unbearable nature of their anxiety symptoms which affect them on physical, mental and spiritual levels of their being. Anxiety is frequently linked to depression and the combination of these two makes the risk of suicide greater especially when the absence of hope in a future recovery is lacking, so that the sufferer feels trapped in his or her unbearable existence.

In later chapters it will be claimed that the Christian faith is able to present a path of hope and liberation from the worst terrors of the anxiety state, though it must be understood it is not an easy route. The effect of anxiety on human relations and, indeed, on our relations with God, is of profound importance. So too is the effect our early relationships have on the degree to which we experience anxiety. To this we now turn.

3
THE ROOTS OF
ANXIETY

If we accept the fact that anxiety is a natural and God-given part of being human and that it can be a spur to creative and energetic living, why is it that for many people it becomes a real burden and for some a waking nightmare? Is it that some people are simply born more anxious than others, in the way that you might have brown eyes rather than blue ones? Is it something you catch from other people like an infectious disease? Or a kind of behaviour you learn in your early impressionable years as when children begin to mimic their parents' mannerisms? Or is it like a prejudice which you pick up as a child and repeat as if it is your own idea of the world?

Well, I expect it may contain elements of all of those things from time to time and I have no doubt you could find someone prepared to argue the case for each one and for many others. What I aim to do in this chapter is to present what, from my study and experience as a counsellor, I believe are the main causes of anxiety. I will begin with our early life as individuals as I am among those who believe that infancy is the single most important factor influencing our adult experience of anxiety. Then I will go on to say something about the way our anxiety levels are affected by the problems and crises we face in adult life and our attitude to the inevitable crisis of death. Finally we will think about the modern world, a world which is always changing very rapidly and which has largely lost its belief in a God who 'holds the whole world in his hands' and consider how that may have increased the underlying depth of anxiety with which we live in our society.

The Development of Anxiety in Infancy

Our very early childhood relationships are extremely important in laying down a good and solid base to our personalities. If this does not go well, we grow up more at risk of suffering deep anxiety in later life. If we have good early relationships it is as if we mentally digest them and they become a part of our inner world, something we can draw on for the rest of our lives to give a solid sense of security. If we have painful, inadequate and insecure early relationships we take those into our inner world and later, even when things are going reasonably well in our lives, below the surface we are always waiting anxiously for bad things to happen.

For these early relationships to be good, they need to be secure and reliable and to give us a reasonable feeling of warmth and love. In practice they may fail to do this adequately either because most of the time the people we depend on are not able, for one reason or another, to provide what we need from them when we are small. Or they succeed most of the time but fail when there is a crisis from which they cannot protect us.

One thing you can say with certainty about a very small baby is that it is totally vulnerable and in need of being looked after. Fortunately this need is so strong in the baby that it produces in most adults an answering urge to pick it up and care for it. If the child is abandoned and not rescued it will surely die because it has not yet developed enough independence to act, other than by the very valuable ability to make a loud and disturbing protest, which usually makes the adult world take notice. Other than that, the baby is totally dependent for its physical survival on other people for food, shelter and a reasonable degree of comfort.

At the same time, the baby has not yet developed any degree of psychological independence, that is to say any sense of being a separate person with a reasonably secure sense of 'self'. Having been literally tied to its mother in the womb, when it is first in the outside world it remains tied to her (or her substitute) in a psychological sense, and this degree of dependency means, as I have said, that the baby is extremely vulnerable to neglect and abandonment.

In his book *Clinical Theology* Frank Lake called this period of most extreme dependency 'the womb of the spirit', suggesting by that name that it is a time of transition and growth which prepares the new-born infant for further independence. Because babies have no spoken language, they rely on the physical senses to feel sure of the presence of the mother (I shall use the term 'mother' to cover anyone who is in that mothering relationship to the child). Her firm but gentle touch, the contact with her eyes and face, the comfort and satisfaction of her milk, all add to the baby's sense of security and love.

Even at this very early stage the baby begins to experience being separate: mother turns away and eye contact is lost and there is a tiny moment of separation; the baby wakes up alone and is uncomfortable and experiences another longer separation but soon begins to cry and someone comes quite quickly before there is too much distress for the child. Slowly longer periods of separation become possible, indeed necessary, so that the child is able to experience him or herself as a separate person. All this is quite a worrying period for some parents as there is no absolute rule about how long to leave the baby crying. Inexperienced parents tend to worry about being too hard or too soft and causing harm. If you had a difficult time as a child yourself and were left far too long in distress and mounting anxiety, you may find you get too anxious now and cannot confidently judge how best to behave. It is important to remember that the child does not need perfect parents but what Donald Winnicott called in his now famous phrase, 'good-enough mothering' in order to develop. Sometimes it is a good idea to get some advice from someone whose experience you trust and act decisively on that advice 'as if', for your child's sake, you actually feel confident.

During this period of dependency the child will naturally feel anxious from time to time just as we, as adults, feel anxious when faced with a new situation or challenge; but the anxiety will hopefully not become too intense and will act as a spur to development, and then die down as the new situation is dealt with or as things return to a more familiar state. But if the circumstances are such that anxiety goes on building up it can reach a level of almost overwhelming intensity which is unbearable and seems to threaten the very existence of the child. This is the level referred to earlier as 'primary anxiety'. In this state the most basic inner self, still in this fragile and dependent stage of development, is threatened with destruction. Although the infant is not actually destroyed, afterwards the memory of this horror is stored away in the hidden cellar of the mind we call the unconscious and the less intense kind of anxiety called 'signal anxiety' is set like one of those security alarms which go off if anyone comes even close to the building it is protecting.

As far as the infant is concerned, it seems there is a variety of experiences which can drive him or her deep into anxiety. I think that loss of the person you are most dependent on is high on the list and, of course, 'loss' means not only actual, permanent loss, like death or abandonment, but the threat of loss when, for example, separation goes on for too long or when there is no explanation given that can explain the loss. Even during later infancy and on through childhood, such loss can cause intense anxiety, though it is generally agreed that the earlier in life the trauma is experienced and the less emotionally developed the child, the more profoundly disturbing is the feeling of anxiety. The older child with 'good-enough' parenting in the early years will have taken inside him or herself enough good and reliable experiences of parents and other important people to draw on and to keep going during the later critical times.

There are many examples of such loss and separation in the histories of sufferers of anxiety:

At two years old Juliet knew her mother was having another baby. They did all they could to prepare her for the birth but mother had to be rushed into hospital when things began to go wrong and, although the new baby was delivered safely, she had to stay in hospital with it for over three weeks. Juliet experienced the sudden disappearance and loss of her mother very anxiously. Nothing much was explained to her by her father. When mother finally returned, it was without the baby which had died in hospital. She was in a deeply depressed state and quite unable to provide the good quality of relationship Juliet needed. Once grown up and married, Juliet could not bear her husband going away without feeling intense anxiety. And later, when she had her own children she became a very possessive mother, always very anxious when they had to go away even for short periods. Eventually she came into therapy to get help.

Early separations which involved hospitals in the days before mothers were able to stay with young children often crop up in the stories of over-anxious people. Ben, mentioned earlier, told me about an experience of his.

Ben began to recognise that he became intensely anxious at the slightest sign of rejection by his wife. This would lead to such anxiety that he could not go away from home and although he knew this was irrational it made no difference. In beginning to talk this through, he linked it to a time twenty-five years before when he was a young man very much in love. His girlfriend had gone abroad promising to come back, only to write and say it was all over. This was upsetting in anyone's book and might have caused sadness and depression but Ben suffered a much more severe break-down of his normal personality and was overpowered by anxiety. Further self-exploration led him earlier into his life when he had been sent away into hospital for a long period as a very young child and it was here that he discovered the roots of his anguish which were so alarmingly aroused by these quite minor rejections by his wife even after twenty years of marriage.

As adults we are able to be alone for a time and feel reasonably safe, though the length of time we can feel comfortable varies from person to person. When we are left alone, say by the person we are closest to, we do not suppose they have gone for ever, because we have many earlier experiences that people come back; we do not suppose they have ceased to exist some-where just because they do not exist in sight and sound of us now; we do not feel utterly powerless to do something, to phone someone or search for them, if they do fail to return before we begin to feel too anxious; finally, we do not feel in danger of falling apart psychologically because we have experience of existing as separate and individual people.

All that will be true for most of us as adults provided the separation is not too long, though you may be someone who, reading this, feels that the period you can stand being alone without strong anxiety is very short indeed. If that is the case, it is almost certain that the roots of it lie in your early, unconsciously-remembered experience: your fear is not so much about something which might happen in the future as a re-experiencing of what has happened in the past.

An important point to remember here is that separation and the sense of loss are not caused only by actual physical separation. Some children experience their parents as so cold, detached and remote that they cannot get from them the sense of warmth and of being loved and valued in the way they need. They may easily feel this lack of goodness is somehow their own fault and feel anxious about their own worth. Or they may feel that the world is such a barren and empty place that they will find nothing good in it to satisfy their needs. Sometimes people will describe their parents in glowing terms as the sort of people who have supplied every possible material need of theirs as children, yet they have felt deprived of the kind of close relationship in which people give not just things but themselves.

I am reminded of watching a young family at a nearby table in a restaurant. The family were mother, father and three daughters aged around 8, 6 and 4. The eldest daughter and the mother seemed separate and self-contained; the middle daughter sparkled attractively at her father and seemed to have all his attention. He seemed quite delighted by her. The youngest girl clearly wanted father's attention too and tried every way to get it. She did not behave badly or make a great noise but every thing she tried, every word she spoke, failed to make her father look at her – he literally had his head turned away towards the middle daughter. I watched this little scene of family life being acted out throughout the meal. The daughter's mounting sense of desperation was obvious. It struck me that it must have seemed to her as if she was invisible, as if she had disappeared and could no longer be seen or heard. Eventually, of course, and after a long time of desperate but still restrained attention-seeking, she went too far and her father turned angrily and told her off before turning away again.

I expect the attention the little girl got from her father would

31

have given her mixed feelings: on the one hand it might have increased her anxiety because she had made him angry and that might lead to him rejecting her even more; on the other hand sometimes even uncomfortable attention is better than no attention at all. No attention might mean you do not exist or are so unimportant and powerless that you are left in a lot of anxiety about yourself. As we have all seen on occasion, some children and some adults choose to be in trouble or at odds with authority most of the time. This may have various causes but not least is the need to get attention as a way of keeping anxiety at bay. Some adults, like the little girl, spend their lives fearing they will die if they cannot get and keep someone's attention.

Naturally, the kind of attention we most want in the first place is approval and one way we can get that as children is by taking careful note of what the powerful adults like and doing what we think will please them. As long as we can do this and not make any waves we hope we can live in peace and security and avoid feeling the awful anxiety their disapproval causes. Of course, in the ordinary way of things, infants growing into childhood and on into adult life have to adapt themselves to what parents in particular and society in general expect of them. But in a healthy family and society, one that is not too rigid, this still gives the child a lot of space for self-expression and play and creativity without the God-given life being crushed out of them. In some families, though, the limits of acceptable behaviour are so narrow that there is hardly room for the child to stretch and grow emotionally. Furthermore, if they do step over the limits they may fear the violent anger it creates or the sense of utter rejection. Often this latter fear is greater. One girl I knew hated her father's angry and unpredictable outbursts, but it was only when he refused to talk to her for several days that she was almost overcome by anxiety.

Although the child's fear of disapproval, punishment and rejection may be partly kept at bay by becoming 'a good little boy or girl', that does not solve the problem of anxiety for them. As we know from the political history of the world as well as from the history of individual people, when we human beings are pushed down and made to be too obedient, our powerful inner instinct to be free and to rebel gets stronger. When it gets very strong, it can feel like a volcano ready to erupt and destroy things in its path. When a child, or later an adult, feels this way it is a cause of further anxiety and, frequently, depression too. And these quite explosive and destructive feelings build up inside, aimed at the very person whose approval is most wanted. Imagine the inner conflict of having very destructive feelings towards the very person on whom you feel most dependent. Sometimes you may feel this towards God: a great deal of anger which you cannot bring yourself to express for fear that you may destroy, if not God, then God's love, so that God may retaliate and destroy you.

The anxiety created by this kind of conflict is bad enough when the parents behave in fairly consistent ways. That is to say they are rigid but fair; the same behaviour is always rewarded, other behaviour is always punished. However, it is so much worse when it is unpredictable and when the child has no idea what has caused the reaction of violent disapproval. In this situation the child's anxiety goes far higher because there is no way in which he or she can control matters by 'good' behaviour.

When Sam was 8 years old, he was given what he wanted most of all for his birthday, an electric train set. He set it out and in the evening showed it to his friends at his party. He was very proud of it and had an exciting time. He caught a slightly disapproving look from his father once or twice when he got too noisy but nothing more. He said,

> 'At the end, when everyone had gone, my dad was really cold. He told me to go straight to bed but I didn't know what I'd done. In the morning everything was normal except the train set had gone. Nobody ever said anything about it and I never saw the train set again. I never said anything but gradually I began to wonder if I'd ever had it at all.'

When Sam was a bit older his father used to take him to football for all home matches. He loved these times less for the football than for being with his dad. They used to joke a lot together and that made Sam feel specially close. One time they got home and Sam made a joke about his father's woolly hat to his mother. His dad didn't laugh as he would normally do when they were out together, he simply left the room and everything fell flat. Nothing was said but Sam was never taken to the match again.

There were other incidents involving Sam's father. Usually the sudden and extreme reaction came when he least expected it and was being most carefree. Not surprisingly Sam has grown up tense and anxious, as he put it, 'waiting for the axe to fall'.

In this example, the father's behaviour does seem unpredictable to his son, though it may be there was an actual pattern in its being a reaction to Sam's excitement. In some cases though the parent's behaviour really has nothing directly to do with the child. Their remoteness or bad temper or unhappiness has other causes. They are worried about work or depressed or unwell but their young child, already anxious and insecure, believes that he or she is the cause of the trouble though powerless to do anything about it. When children live with parents who are very anxious and emotionally unstable, who behave in unpredictable and extreme ways, they are likely to grow up very anxious themselves.

When as adults we become parents and think we recognise the mistakes our parents have made, we will often make a deliberate attempt to put things right for our own children. Sometimes, of course, we over-compensate and get it wrong in the other direction.

Child Abuse

For some children anxiety is generated not so much by subtle forms of parental neglect and the parents' failure to be available in a loving way, but by actual physical or sexual abuse. In recent years, particularly, it has become obvious just how common the sexual abuse of children has been in our society and it is obvious to anyone working with such children or with adults who have carried the burden of such abuse for many years just how deeply anxious they are.

In both forms of abuse the adult world fails miserably to protect the child in a secure way especially at a time when they are most dependent and vulnerable. This is true most of all when the abuser is someone in the close circle of family relationships and particularly so when it is one or both of the parents: those people appointed by God to be the child's chief protectors and providers. This produces a massive conflict within the child between dependency, on the one hand, and fear and outrage about what is being done to them on the other.

In the case of direct physical abuse (by which I mean injury of a non-sexual kind) the attacker may leave no doubt about his or her intention or the anger and violence which drives them. Sometimes the attack on the child is calculated and cold-blooded but at other times it is very wild and hot-blooded. It is all too clear from the dreadful injuries we have all heard reported in the press that sometimes the child is faced with an adult who, at least for that moment, is totally out of control and overwhelmed by the most primitive destructive impulses, and this is a terrifying experience for the child. It may be that the attack is directly on the child but sometimes it is on someone else in the family, maybe father attacking mother or another child, and this too can be a harrowing experience. These attacks produce in the child feelings of fear and violent anger towards the attacker which can be almost as overwhelmingly strong as the feelings they are seeing in the other person. The child may feel murderous and wants to retaliate but cannot strike back because of his or her own vulnerability or that of others in the family, especially if the violent attacker is the father or someone of equal importance. Consequently these powerful feelings of terror and anger become swallowed and a legacy of anxiety is left behind. As the child grows up into adolescence and adulthood, this anxiety may give way to violently angry feelings which hit out at almost anyone who is thought to be at all threatening.

In the case of sexual abuse another important factor may enter the equation when the abuser is in the close family circle: it is the confusing element of seduction. Attack is more honest in showing its destructiveness. Seduction presents a more smiling face and more soothing words. Whatever is being done to the child, especially a very young and unknowing child, may be presented as something pleasant and loving. Indeed there may be a lot of confusion in the child about whether this is nice or not. He or she may experience some pleasurable sensations and at first like the special closeness and attention which goes with it. However, the sexual activity is grossly inappropriate for the child and deeply disturbing and there is soon, if not at once, a growing sense of unease, fear and disgust. Further anxiety is linked with the need for secrecy which is required of the child by threats or emotional blackmail. This secrecy and the constant fear of discovery adds greatly to the burden of anxiety. If it is the father who is abusing his daughter, she frequently fears that the whole family will be destroyed if the hidden abuse becomes known, so that preserving her family has to come first.

Once again there is a situation of considerable conflict between opposing inner forces. This conflict cannot easily be resolved so it is pushed underground and the victim is left prone to the kind of anxiety which will reappear at later stages in her life.

Anxiety like this can be made even worse by hidden guilt: the child fears that it is their own natural sexual feelings or their desire to have a specially close and even exclusive relationship with one of their parents which has somehow brought about the awful situation, when the reality is that the abuser has been guilty of breaking a most precious trust. Because of such unwarranted guilt, in later life, the victim, most commonly a woman, may feel that her sexuality is bad and dangerous and to be kept heavily under control. Such a person may find that her attraction to anyone else or their attraction to her provokes anxiety in her which can only be calmed down by withdrawing from the situation. She may make herself in some way unattractive in order to ward off the likelihood of gaining attention. As one young woman said, 'I grew fat and I grew spots to keep men away'. All men may become tarred with the same brush in the mind of the abused girl so that every man is an abuser waiting to strike and the adult woman cannot let herself begin to trust any man for fear of the abuse being repeated. She does not so much suspect that it might be repeated as know deep inside her that it *will* be repeated sooner or later. This anxiety may show itself in the form of nervousness and hesitancy or, like any anxiety, may be expressed in hatred and aggression.

Stages of Development

As we grow from earliest childhood up through the years to mature adulthood we have to face a number of psychological turning points which can seem like so many hurdles, each one a potential source of anxiety. In our earliest years we have to learn to gain control over our own bodies and our turbulent inner feelings; we develop basic skills like speaking and walking and making good relationships within the family, which often includes dealing with feelings of jealousy and envy towards sisters and brothers. Later we have to move out of the security of the family and make our way in the world of school and peer relationships, learning to co-operate and compete satisfactorily. In adolescence there is the critical phase of sexual development which is particularly prone to throw up anxieties, some of which have their roots much earlier in life. The young person has to accept the obvious physical changes of puberty and the powerful sexual emotions and sensations which go along with them, come to terms with their emerging adult sexual identity, and begin to form what will become, in time, adult sexual relationships. This is all very exciting and stimulating for many people but for others who are ill-informed or already carrying the weight of personal insecurity or their parents' failure to come to terms with their own sexuality, it can be a nightmare of anxiety. Sometimes they will attempt to escape in one way or another by denying their sexual confusion but this puts down a layer of anxiety which remains a deep insecurity throughout life or until it is resolved.

Adolescence also includes the big social hoops of examinations and choices about careers and work or, indeed, unemployment. One way or another it means making the transition from the world of childhood and education into the grown-up work-centred world. For some this is a more painful transition than they are prepared for; some have not realised the extent to which they have been protected from the harsher and more uncertain aspects of the adult world by virtue of remaining like children to a fairly advanced stage. Some parents have done their children a disservice by failing to help them make the gradual separation over the years.

One glaring example of this failure on the part of a father to prepare his son gradually for independence was told to me some years ago.

The young boy growing up through childhood and adolescence had everything he needed provided for him but he was not allowed to have any money of his own. When he began a paper-round as a teenager he had to hand over the money to his father who handed back small amounts for whatever the boy needed. Even when he began work, still under the dominance of his father, he was required to hand over his pay packet so that his father could control his finances. He said, 'The day I was 21 it all stopped. I was told I had to look after the money myself. My dad said, "You're on your own now." It was the most terrifying day of my life.'

Of course what is at issue is not so much the financial dependency but the psychological dependency which underlies it so that the young man, even when he is a working 'man', resists opposing his father and claiming his right to self-control. His terror is that he will be punished and abandoned, which eventually he is. Sadly, of course, some fail to make any real separation at all even well into adult life.

Even as an adult woman June did everything she possibly could with her mother. Father had died when she was twelve, though they were already seen by friends to be very, very close. When they had to be apart they kept in touch constantly by phone. If June went somewhere for the evening, she would phone the moment she arrived at her friend's; quite often her mother would find some excuse to phone during the course of the evening; June would phone again just before she left to come home. If there was a hold-up on the way back, she would phone yet again. (This was in the days before the mobile phone. It occurs to me they would have loved that piece of technology.) Their deep dependency and attachment to each other was even more clear in that if I asked June what she thought on any subject she would answer, 'Mother thinks . . .'. It was almost impossible to get a separate reply.

As you may guess, June made no close relationships other than the one with her mother. Certainly she made no sexual relationships and, as far as I am aware, experienced no sexual desire. She shared a bedroom with her mother even though there were other rooms available in the house.

June was suffering from chronic anxiety when I met her. Her mother had died two years before and life without her was totally unreal to June. She was on a heavy dose of tranquillisers and seemed to live a kind of half-life. She thought of suicide as a way of ending her suffering and reuniting with her mother. She said, 'When my mother died, I died.'

I think that was probably true. Perhaps she had never been properly alive; had never finished getting born.

Both these examples of failure to separate satisfactorily are quite extreme cases but, of course, the same thing goes on in lesser and more subtle ways many times over. It is not just a failure of the parents to let go or just a failure of the growing child to move on. It is an attempt by both to avoid the anxiety of separation and loss though, of course, it causes much greater anxiety in the long term than it avoids in the short term.

Although this process of growing up and getting successfully through a number of developmental hoops may cause anxiety at various stages, when we do get through them we are able to move ahead confidently. However, we may get stuck, and this leads to more overwhelming anxiety; or we avoid facing our problems and fears and succeed only in burying them out of sight. In such cases we are left with a legacy of anxiety which may return at a later date. It is worth repeating that, generally speaking, the earlier in life things go wrong, the more severe is the underlying anxiety and the more difficult we find it to cope with crises in later life. To change the picture from hoops to building blocks and to borrow an analogy from the Christian gospel, you can imagine the earliest experiences of good, secure and reliable relationships laying down a firm foundation upon which other blocks will be laid in the months and years ahead. If those later blocks are not well laid and feel unsteady, that causes a degree of anxiety, but the whole structure is not threatened with collapse. If, on the other hand, the very foundations are profoundly insecure, whatever is built on them is in constant threat and the whole edifice is at risk. Then the unfortunate individual is in danger of suffering the worst kind of anxiety and terror especially when later circumstances shake them.

4
ADULT CRISES

When we are growing up we look towards adult life as a sort of plateau that we will eventually reach. There we imagine the ground is fairly level and life is secure and stable and that we will have considerable power and freedom. When we actually get to that stage ourselves, we may find the going far from smooth and there can be periods of disturbance in our circumstances or inside ourselves which leave us feeling like powerless children, anxious and needy. Here life produces for us more developmental hoops for us to get through. We discover that we have arrived at adulthood not as a final destination but merely at a certain stage of a greater journey. For the Christian, at least for one who has been adequately taught, this is not too disturbing, as the whole of life is understood in the context of a larger framework.

This being said, there is still truth in the notion that psychologically we level out as we move into adult life. In the early days, months and years of life the stages of development are quite close together and change is rather rapid, whereas in adult life the times between the major changes lengthen quite a lot.

Some people who have grown up with 'good-enough' early relationships, who have not suffered from crises that they could not cope with and who have found a satisfying faith or philosophy of life, will reach the adult years with a high degree of positive feeling and appetite for life. (One hopes they will also be without the arrogance that over-protection can instil.) They will be fairly open personalities and not heavily defended against emotional closeness and involvement with other people. You would expect them to feel anxiety in the normal course of events but not to an unreasonable degree.

Others, who have had to deal with situations and relationships which have provoked a lot of anxiety will, nevertheless, have managed to develop strong and effective defences so that their personalities appear secure and for the most part they are able to face life without being troubled by much anxiety. (Later I will describe some of the more common defences we use to keep anxiety at bay.) The problem for them may be that their defences limit, to some degree, their freedom to be as open and creative as they might wish. Being highly defensive emotionally is like wearing a suit of armour: it is very good for deflecting 'the slings and arrows of outrageous fortune' but it rather limits your style if you want to dance or make love.

Others, who have had to deal with excessive early anxiety will have developed defences which are more extreme and their behaviour may appear to other people as distinctly 'odd' in one way or another. These defences may work quite well as a means of stopping them from feeling over-anxious, but they live an emotionally and spiritually impoverished life, a life that may seem empty and meaningless.

Yet others, who have had to face early and excessive anxiety will have failed somehow to develop defences in any way strong enough to contain their anxiety with the result that, even with a restricted way of life, they are almost constantly the victims of anxiety and feel on edge and panicky.

Within this broad range of defensiveness there are many degrees. Psychologically we are all defensive to some extent but within society some defensiveness is more or less normal whilst the same basic thing in a more extreme form is regarded as peculiar. For example, keeping your house clean and tidy is practical and 'normal' behaviour. You might say it is a defence against disease and chaos and against the anxiety you would feel if things got out of hand. Now some people, if they are worried and edgy about something not at all connected with the cleaning will tidy up the house even if it is reasonably neat already. They will straighten the cushions or dust the sideboard and they somehow feel calmed and more secure as if they have regained some control over whatever was worrying them. (I am suddenly reminded of the day following my father's unexpected death: I came down early in the morning to find my mother energetically cleaning through the house as if that could repair the tragedy that had occurred.) When their anxiety is past they may laugh at themselves for their 'neurotic' behaviour and other people they tell will chip in with what they do to allay their anxiety. People do not think this is too crazy and are relieved that others do the same. At a more extreme end of the defensive scale are people who spend a good part of each day slavishly re-cleaning and retidying the house as their only means of keeping at bay what-ever, in their inner world, threatens to overwhelm them if they let up for a moment. As a defence it may work quite effectively but at a cost to the individual and the family who may feel tyrannised by the compulsive cleaner.

Wherever we are on the emotionally defensive scale, most of us reach the start of adulthood coping one way or another with the demands and responsibilities of life. In other words our personalities are sufficiently together to manage. Some of us manage with real or apparent ease, others of us with a great deal of struggle and support. Some are still very much caught up in the earlier developmental hoops and need a level of parenting that would suit a child rather than a person of adult age; but the vast majority of us cope one way or another, as long as things are going reasonably well and the structure of life we have created around us stays in place. This 'structure' includes other people and things in our outside world which we depend upon and feel attached to. It also includes personal qualities. If you think about your own life you can no doubt make a fairly long list of things which you rely on for a sense of security and well-being. High on the list for most people will be close personal relationships, family, a job or some other social status, a home, savings, perhaps a car and other possessions. It may include the wider social and political context that gives stability to life and, certainly for some, it will include high on the agenda their philosophy of life and their religious faith. The list will also include a wide range of personal qualities: good health, sexual attractiveness, intelligence, special talents, orderliness, self-control, loyalty, generosity and so on; qualities which we think or hope we possess and which, to a greater or lesser degree, we depend on for our sense of security and worth. It may be interesting for you to make your list and then to prune it right down to the five or six items that it would be really difficult for you to lose.

It is often loss of these things (I include people and qualities in that word) or the threatened loss of them which brings about a personal crisis which lays us open to attacks of anxiety. Some of these losses occur in the natural course of growing older: the loss of a youthful body or physical endurance or the loss of freedom upon taking up increased responsibility; in later middle life, the loss of grown-up children leaving home or the loss of the older generation as they begin to die in old age. Later still there is the loss of status upon retirement and possibly the loss of some faculties which comes with age. Each stage of loss may be accompanied by anxiety and depression, though how deep and how long-lasting this will be varies according to how dependent we have been on whatever was lost and how vulnerable we are to anxiety on the basis of our early experiences.

Imagine, for example, a girl who grows up in her early years feeling very unloved and insecure. She finds that she is repeatedly ignored and cannot get close to her rather withdrawn father. In her teens she develops very attractively and is never without the attention of admirers. She enjoys this new-found power and for the first time does not live with a constant underlying fear of being isolated and ignored. On the contrary she seems to grow up with a considerable degree of self-confidence. However, the process of having babies, the appearance of stretch-marks and the effects of breast feeding cause her considerable anxiety. She becomes convinced, however much he denies it, that her husband no longer finds her attractive and cannot believe that he finds anything else about her, other than her physical attractiveness, at all important. She watches for every new line that appears on her face with increasing desperation as if her whole being depends on the texture of her skin. It appears that she greatly fears the future, and in a sense she does, but you could say she fears, much more, the past and a return to the feelings of insecurity and isolation from which she escaped.

Or imagine the experience of two mothers in middle age whose youngest children, now adult, are leaving home and moving away. One mother is devastated by the intense feeling of loss and cannot get over it for a long time. The other mother feels some sadness at the passing of a phase in her life but, far from being devastated, feels pleased to see her offspring making their own way in the world and rather relishes the greater personal freedom the change will bring for her. This second mother, we imagine, has a sound sense of security and is not desperately dependent on certain other people to hold her world together. The first mother, though, has carried from childhood a deep feeling of insecurity and loneliness which she has solved for herself by having a child whom she has kept very close to her from birth. She suffered a depression when the child first went off to school and now, with this greater loss, her anxiety breaks through. She suffers not only the current loss but all the feeling of loss she has carried inside for forty years.

Or imagine the man or woman whose whole sense of worth is tied up in work. Within the confines of the workshop or office they know what their role is, they are competent and confident and have the respect of colleagues and subordinates. But underneath, as people, they feel anxious and inadequate. As long as their role is maintained, their defences against anxiety hold, but their eventual and inevitable retirement shakes the structure of their lives as they lose the things they have most relied upon. It may even be that their crisis comes earlier as changes in technology or styles of management make their skills redundant so they lose what confidence and competence they had.

In addition to these changes which come with the passing of the years there are, of course, the less predictable crises which may shake the very foundations of life so that the defences cannot contain the underlying anxiety. The most obvious example of this is the death of someone you are specially close to and dependent upon. In any close relationship such a loss will naturally mean a lengthy period of grief and mourning (unless the grief is unnaturally suppressed) but in some people its effects are so great and it causes or threatens such a collapse that they totally suppress the grief or cannot come to terms with it at all. In the most extreme cases life may feel so intolerable that suicide seems the only way out of the unbearable pain.

Other unexpected crises which shake the foundations include divorce, redundancy, financial and business failure, traumatic accidents, serious physical injury and disability and so forth. The degree to which we are affected, as I have said before, depends in a large measure on the degree of our psychological dependency on whatever is lost.

At a spiritual and psychological level, these sudden crises, as well as the more predictable crises I mentioned before, are always a challenge to further growth and development. Every crisis means some form of loss but it also means the possibility of discovering and gaining something new. In most cases this working through is achieved with the support of family, friends, the church and community, but in some cases, especially when the emotional conflicts and inadequacies of early life are triggered off by adult situations, people may need more special help. I shall return to this subject in the final chapter.

Wider Issues

What has been said so far in this and the previous chapter has mainly concentrated on the fairly immediate circumstances of the individual, and how anxiety may be heightened by early relationships and later experiences. But it is worth bearing in mind that our individual experiences are set against a much wider background. The period since the Second World War has often been referred to as 'the age of anxiety' (a phrase first coined by the poet W.H. Auden), indicating a general increase in anxiety, at least in the developed world. It is beyond the scope of this book to explore these wider issues in any detail but I want to refer to three things which I think are most important.

The first is the tremendous increase in scientific knowledge and technology which gives us undreamed-of power over life and death on a global scale. This power also means a sense of tremendous responsibility which most of us are not at all confident we can handle. At the same time the few who are confident they can handle matters, the politicians, do not always inspire a matching confidence in us. We know pretty well how to use power destructively and fear we will not be able to stop ourselves from doing so either by sudden nuclear conflict or the more gradual processes of global warming and pollution. We know that the power is there in a technological sense to be creative, but this requires a degree of spiritual and psychological maturity and a level of trust and sympathetic communication which we know we find difficult on a personal level let alone an international one.

This is linked with my second point which is the widespread loss of faith in a God who actively intervenes in world affairs and carries ultimate responsibility for what happens. Although some people both inside and outside organised religion do still believe in a God like that, most, I suspect, do not and therefore cannot find comfort in the belief that once prevailed widely that obedience to God's law offered a guarantee of security. We sometimes feel like children who have been under the protection of a father who is fair even if rather demanding and suddenly find ourselves behind the wheel of his powerful car without the certainty that we can drive. We need a mature and co-operative relationship with this father/God to contain our anxiety and to work out how we are to use our power.

The third point, linked to the above, is the sheer speed of change and technological development in the modern world. This adds a feeling of urgency to the need we have to gain and maintain control. The speed of change is increasingly difficult for people as they age and find themselves less and less familiar with much of the world around them. In the elderly this can easily produce a sense of alienation from their society with all the attendant anxiety that brings.

As with the personal changes I mentioned before, these wider-reaching changes in the world and the anxiety they cause can be a spur to human development. What is needed are qualities which go beyond the desire for personal comfort and individual survival which so often motivate us; qualities which, though not peculiar to Christianity, are part and parcel of it.

Fear of Death

The only certainty about our earthly life, and the final transition we have to make, is death, and this is the focus for a great deal of anxiety. Much of this anxiety remains unconscious and is avoided by denial and other forms of defence so that we do not think about it or, if occasionally we are forced to think about it, we try to push it away as quickly as possible. We cannot avoid acknowledging death as a fact of life – to do so would be irrational and unrealistic – but that kind of acknowledgement is a far cry from a genuine acceptance of its reality. As one lady of fifty-eight said to me, 'Now I've been told my father is dying, I realise, for the first time, I have to accept my parents' mortality. It's ridiculous but I know I have never done that. It was as if they would live for ever.' Such a denial of mortality for this woman is a denial of her own mortality and of her fear of separation and annihilation.

As we have seen, the fear of separation from the people and things that give our lives security, meaning and satisfaction is the cause of much anxiety, and death is, in our human existence, the most complete and final separation. If we are still desperately dependent on certain people and things for our sense of being, their potential loss through their death or our own death will cause intense anxiety and in some cases may produce a reaction of fear at the very mention of the word.

Where there is a deeply dependent relationship, the fear of separation through death may lead to considering the extreme measure of suicide if the loved one dies. For example, the young parents of a baby who died a cot death talked together about which of them might commit suicide to join the child beyond the grave so the child would not be alone. A middle-aged man attempted suicide when his parents died because life without them was intolerable. A woman successfully killed herself soon after the death of her husband in an attempt to be reunited with him. In these cases and in many others the fear of your own death may not prove as strong as the intolerable pain of separation and loss. In these situations the continuation of life and the awfulness of existence in isolation may overcome any anxiety about death itself.

On the other hand, people who suffer chronically from very high levels of anxiety and have become depressed and despairing because they see no hope of release from their pain may also consider suicide, and occasionally carry it out, not in the hope that it will reunite them with loved ones but in the hope that death is simply non-existence, a state of non-being in which there is no consciousness and, therefore, no pain. But, of course, they cannot be sure.

The very uncertainty surrounding death is the cause of considerable anxiety. Whilst death itself is inevitable, how and when we will die and, particularly, what being dead will be like cannot be answered with any certainty. We cannot attempt to calm our anxiety, as we may in other situations, by talking to someone who has done it before us to find out all the details, neither can we think ourselves into the situation and plan how we will deal with particular problems as they arise as we might do facing some other unfamiliar situation. As we all try to lower our anxiety, one way or another, by exercising self-control and imposing order on the world around us, we feel specially vulnerable at the prospect of death when control slips away. This is particularly true for some people of a rather obsessional character. For them the thought of dying itself and the inevitable loss of control it involves is horrifying. In practice, when there is a prolonged terminal illness, this anxiety may be worked through so that the patient is able to accept the passive role their illness forces on them and allow themselves to be held and supported by the love and care of other people. They may then experience a depth of peace and spiritual maturity which is amazing to their family and friends.

As to what lies beyond death, we can have no certainty of the kind that can be scientifically tested but only that knowledge which relies on faith, belief or supposition. People have various ideas about life after death. Viewed psychologically these ideas seem to fulfil some basic need in the individual, a need which is related not just to death but to their whole life. One view, held by a lot of people, is that death will mean a reunion with people who have died already. They hope to find that, in the final analysis, there is no separation, no loss of the particular individuals they have loved. (Occasionally this belief about reunion carries a sting in the tail. Some people dread that they will be reunited with somebody whose earlier death was a great relief for them, setting them free from an abusive relationship. They fear that when their turn comes to die they will have to face the dreaded person all over again and there will never be any escape.)

The view of life after death held by some other people is dominated by the idea of judgement. Now, although from a Christian point of view God's judgement of us is well founded in scripture and theology, the view I am referring to is a distortion of that belief. It is distorted in that it sees only the negative, guilt-ridden side of judgement. Deep down, if not consciously, God is seen as hard and punitive, and those who hold this view often believe themselves to be bad and deserving punishment. They are dominated by a harsh inner parent which they project onto God whom they make into a sadistic being. Such an idea of God is a far cry from the qualities of fatherly love and mercy which are the hallmarks of a Christ-centred view of God. The thought of

49

such a death may well provoke anxiety but, paradoxically, some people have a need for punishment and feel they can have no rest until their punishment is complete.

I must add that others whose view of life after death is dominated by the idea of judgement see badness, not in themselves, whom they feel to be victims of life-long injustice, but in other people. They rather relish the hope that others will get their come-uppance at the hands of the Almighty.

A further idea about life beyond death is that there is none. That is to say, some people hold to the view that beyond death is total and complete non-existence. As there is no consciousness, there is no pain, suffering or any continuation of the life they have found to be intolerable on earth. Their anxiety about death may chiefly be the fear that their belief will prove to be false and that it does not provide the escape they long for. To say the least, such a hope for non-existence is a picture of despair in the value and meaning of life and can only be confronted and changed by the discovery of faith and love.

Yet others hold a variety of ideas about heaven, for example those based on the continuation of whatever has given greatest pleasure in this life, like the Anglican bishop who says there must be cricket in heaven as it simply would not be heaven for him without cricket. This is a nice, comforting idea and has a certain no-nonsense quality to set against our anxious uncertainty, but it is clearly in the realm of hope and supposition and has no other authority.

Christianity does not meet our anxiety about death and what lies beyond with the detailed information we might like to satisfy our lust for certainty. As well as judgement the New Testament speaks about resurrection, about renewed life coming out of death. But how and when and where? St Paul writes about our 'spiritual bodies' but what does that mean? And as to 'when', Jesus makes clear he has no information to give.

On the subject of death, as in all else at the end of the day, Christianity offers us not the certainty of knowledge but faith in the nature and love of God to set against our anxious souls.

5
DEFENCES AGAINST ANXIETY

When anxiety gets too much for us early in life, so that we are very distressed and may even feel in danger of being over-whelmed by it, we develop what analysts call 'psychological defences' as a means of survival. This is not a thought-out plan of action but something we do unconsciously and automatically. It becomes part and parcel of our whole personality and colours the way we are most of the time. It is particularly strong, of course, when we are in an unusually stressful situation and anxiety is threatening to break out. On the other hand, it can be far less intense when, for a period of time, we feel safe and relaxed. We may make light of something or make a joke about it when a situation is too threatening, or we may change the subject every time the conversation hovers close to a disturbing topic. We may rely on fantasy or a blind optimism to hide from those realities which make us too apprehensive. All these strategies have their uses in helping us to get through fear, especially when it is well outside any realistic means of our control. But if we spend our whole lives in such avoidance it is a sad matter.

In this chapter I want to describe and illustrate four common ways we may use to defend ourselves against feeling too anxious, not just in the short term, like staying away from a tense situation, but as a lifetime way of living and relating to the world around us. A word of warning: the illustrations offered show a particular aspect of personality and should not be taken to represent the whole person in all their complexity. To some extent, this goes for all the examples in the book but I make the point here to avoid any tendency to think of people only in terms of a particular defence or problem, as when people say, 'She's a depressive' or 'He's an hysteric'. In practice individuals may use a number of different defences at different times or in combination. In any event, people are much more than the sum total of their defences.

You will also notice that each of the defences I describe is quite 'normal' in the sense that most people feel or act that way to some degree at one time or another. As you read on you may find yourself saying, to each one in turn, 'I sometimes feel and behave just like that. Am I being highly neurotic?' Remember that it is only when one or more of these defences become extreme or a very fixed way of relating to the world that it becomes a real problem.

In the same way that some level of anxiety is perfectly normal, so everybody relies on psychological defences as part and parcel of their personality. The problem with these defences is that there is always a price to pay in terms of a loss of energy and freedom. If the defence is too extreme or too rigid, the price can be far too high to be worth it. Imagine I build a low brick wall around my house to stop my neighbours walking across my flower-beds and glancing in through my windows; I have erected a useful 'defence' with which I am quite comfortable. The gate is only on a latch and callers have easy access. However, imagine I begin to feel threatened by an irritating or aggressive newcomer; I build the wall higher and put a lock on the gate. I am safer but I have cut down on my view of the surrounding area and callers, even if they are friends, have more difficulty visiting so they begin to call less often. Perhaps I fear that quite violent groups are moving into the area and I build my walls even higher than the eaves of the house, I replace the gate with a solid, reinforced door. I am safe once more but I dare not go out from my isolated castle. The price in terms of lost freedom may be worth it as long as there is real danger outside but I may find myself locked in and half forgotten even when reasonable safety returns outside. Some people come for counselling because they have lost the key and the lock has rusted over.

As I go on to describe these common defences, I shall highlight with each one the particular price that has to be paid in terms of a loss to human fulfilment if the defence becomes too great. These are by no means comprehensive or exclusive to each type of defence but are intended to be a general indication of how one thing leads to another in emotional terms.

Attachment

Especially when severe anxiety in early life comes about as the result of the child being cut off physically or emotionally from the very people it depends on, some people may develop a way of attaching themselves to others in an attempt to avoid ever again being in that dreadful state of near panic. This is not done as a conscious plan but becomes an automatic way of life. They may feel quite high levels of signal anxiety a lot of the time so that they live very much on the edge of their nerves and are hypersensitive to quite small mood changes in the people around. This alertness is needed to avoid the risk of separation, rejection and isolation which could trigger the awful collapse into primary anxiety. This sort of defence is not so much like the wall described above as like the sensitive alarm system used in many department stores where the expensive coats or electrical goods are wired together and set off loud bells whenever contact is even slightly broken.

George developed severe pains in his legs six weeks after his wife gave birth to their first child. The doctors could find no physical cause though the problem was bad enough for him to have time off work. His wife was put under pressure by the need to look after her husband as well as care for the baby. George was very apologetic at being in the way and insisted that he could do things for himself despite his pain, but something in his voice always left his wife feeling guilty so she still ended up waiting on him. The baby's feeds and bath-time were constantly interrupted by urgent demands from George which left his wife understandably frustrated.

On one occasion when she was delayed for nearly an hour at the baby clinic, George became intensely anxious as he waited at home. When she came back and wanted to talk about her own frustration at being kept waiting, George felt he could not tolerate it, because what he craved from her was not an account of her problems but apologies, sympathy and reassurance; so he accused her of not caring about him. When this led, inevitably, to harsh words, George left the house, despite his painful legs, and visited his mother who poured her usual sympathy on his tears and urged him to stay overnight.

When he eventually went home to his wife he felt anxious that she might be cold and distant so he took an expensive gift and anticipated her every need for two or three days. He kept hugging her and saying how much he loved her and pleaded with her repeatedly to reassure him of her love. She did this, despite a growing irritation, more for a quiet life than for true affection.

This picture of George shows a number of the typical characteristics of someone using attachment as a way of keeping anxiety at bay. His emotional attachment to his wife is such that he needs to be the centre of all her attention. He has always felt threatened by her other relationships with friends, family and work-mates, and the new baby poses a special threat. He is intensely jealous, fearing that the child will depose him from being king of the emotional castle and this throws him into desperate concern. His physical pains, which are real pains even though they have no physical cause, are, of course, a symptom of his anxiety and provide him with a reason for staying close to home and an excuse for competing with his baby for his wife's attention.

Also typical of this kind of behaviour is that George's demands are often manipulative rather than straightforward. He lets his wife know what he wants whilst saying that he will do it himself. At the same time he lets her know by his tone of voice or gesture that he expects her to do it for him. He cannot trust that anyone will really care about him though he wants it to appear that it is they who are insisting on helping him.

His need for the reassurance of love is constant and he equates love with togetherness. Love, for George, is never having to be alone. Being separate, even recognising he is a separate and individual person, is too full of anxiety to be accepted. When he is at odds with his wife, he feels the distance between them and rushes back to his mother, whom he has never really left, to feel like her child once again. And when he returns to his own wife, he has to work hard to get her to reassure him of her love in a desperate attempt to paper over the cracks of their differences. He lives in a state of constant emotional vigilance.

Most people live by attachment to some extent but when it is extreme, as with George, they pay a high price. They lose the experience of being a person in their own right and the experience of solitude as something of value and beauty. Although they look for security in other people and feel desperate to be loved, they cannot trust themselves, other people or God enough to experience a genuinely satisfying love. Emotionally they cannot rest and so know what it is to have contentment and peace.

The cost of letting go the stranglehold of this attachment is by coming face to face with the anxiety which provokes it. This is possible only when a person has the containment of a secure relationship with someone who cannot be successfully manipulated.

Detachment

The second defensive position is at the opposite pole to the first, though in some ways it is closer than it might at first seem. It is well illustrated by the image of the wall used in the introduction, the wall which keeps the world locked outside so that no anxiety-provoking dangers can invade. At the same time there is a deep dungeon under the house into which certain feelings and experiences have been banished and concreted over for fear that they will betray the person from within.

This defence works by cutting off those very feelings and desires for loving and dependable relationships which were severely neglected or threatened early on in life, so leading to the experience of primary anxiety. It is as if we are saying, 'I have eliminated my hunger so completely that I will not know I am starving or fear that I might starve to death.'

Arthur was forty when he married Diane. They met at the library where they both worked and discovered a common interest in collecting and categorising moths and butterflies. Arthur had lived a bachelor life since going to university; he had lived alone and wanted it that way. He had considered sharing a flat but thought having someone else about the place would simply limit his freedom and disturb the quiet routine of his existence. He liked reading, listening to some classical music and, of course, he had his passion for the butterflies. The only blot on his landscape was an occasional feeling of emptiness and a sense that life was quite pointless. He could not understand the will to live against all odds which he saw in the starving and suffering people who appeared on his television screen. He thought he would kill himself under their circumstances.

His relationship with Diane developed very slowly. He admired her mind and her cool self-sufficiency. She never rushed him and seemed not to suffer the unpredictable mood swings he saw and despised in most women. As he approached forty he began to consider the future and the problems of a lonely old age and asked Diane to marry him. In theory Arthur accepted the sexual duties of marriage and physically he performed perfectly well, though the whole business was rather mechanical to his way of thinking and he always felt as if he was simply watching himself from the end of the bed. What distressed him was that his wife became strongly aroused sexually and he saw a side of her personality which made him feel almost terrified. He was similarly disturbed on the few occasions he found her crying and would go for a walk by himself to give her time to calm down and get 'proper control of herself'.

Arthur is a typically detached personality in several ways. Firstly you will notice how he is out of touch with himself, especially from his feelings and emotions. He has got these well damped down and some are quite buried and forgotten in the dungeon of his mind. He lives mainly through his intellect. He relies on what he thinks about things not what he feels. He does not really feel anything strongly. If you ask him, or anybody like him, 'What are you *feeling*?' he will tell you what he is *thinking*. It is not that he is covering up. He is genuinely puzzled if you go on asking about his feelings because he thinks he has already replied.

Arthur's consuming interest is in books and in his special subject, butterflies. It is not that there is anything odd about reading or having a hobby, but for him these solitary pursuits fill a void in his life. He does not have to rely on anyone else and feel the anxiety of being dependent. He never wants to be dependent, ever, on anyone. This is the second way in which he is detached.

He is detached and withdrawn from deep and intimate relationships with other people.

A third way in which he is detached is from some of the physical rhythms and sensations of his body. He does not get any pleasure from movement or dance. In fact physical closeness to other people makes him uncomfortable and he would find it almost impossible, even if he thought of it, to put his arm affectionately around a friend. Even when you shake hands with Arthur, his arm feels like a rigid pole holding you at bay. (Shaking hands with some detached people feels the opposite, as if you have hold of almost nothing.)

Arthur managed to cope with the sexual part of his marriage by keeping himself split in half; leaving his body to perform in a mechanical way but staying outside it like an observer. If you sometimes behave in detached ways yourself, you will find that easy to recognise. On the other hand you may find it impossible to understand. In any event, it worked well enough for Arthur except that the passionate and emotional side of his wife, aroused by their love-making, which he had never suspected to exist, was something he could not handle. Indeed, it terrified him as it began to penetrate the walls of his detachment and feel like a threat to his very existence. His unconscious response to this crisis of anxiety was to become impotent. This problem allowed him to avoid sex with his wife with the result that he did not have to face up to one of the major causes of his anxiety. But of course it created other problems.

Most people use detachment from certain feelings as a way of civilised living but, when it becomes extreme, a high price is paid for security. Awful anxiety may be cut off, but so too will be some of the things which give life depth and meaning: warmth, intimacy and love. Such people cannot let themselves go, laugh at themselves, cry and be vulnerable in ways that bring them into deep and more satisfying touch with other people. People who are emotionally detached often feel life to be meaningless and look for meaning in intellectual ways, only to find that that does not satisfy. It is rather like reading the score for a piece of music when what is really needed is to hear the music played.

Very often, those who keep themselves secure by pushing people away find that they also begin to look down on others, feeling superior as well as detached. They may even begin to despise the 'little people' for their simple beliefs and their simple pleasures although, if they could look deep inside themselves, they would find a hidden longing to be able simply to join in. But somehow they cannot. They are paralysed. Obviously, if they have needed to become extremely detached, it is because they have been desperately hurt at some stage and they will be anxious and resistant to relaxing their defences. Even so it is possible to work for their release.

Obsessional Control

If you ever make lists of the things you have to do when you are busy, you will understand the basic nature of this way of coping with anxiety. It is again the case of a perfectly normal and practical piece of behaviour exaggerated to become a defence against unreasonable fear. When you are too busy and worry that you will not get all your jobs done, making a list and ticking tasks off as you complete them is a simple and effective way of getting on top of things. It calms down your feeling that things might get out of hand. It lets you feel in control. Much of civilised life, through laws and systems, is designed to maintain a reasonable level of control where we can live with each other in reasonable safety. But if a civilisation becomes too controlling, life becomes hardly worth living and certainly loses its joy.

In some people the need to feel in control is very urgent: muddle and disorder, even if it is quite mild disorder, seems to them like the onset of total chaos. This signals anxiety and their immediate, spontaneous reaction is for greater, if not absolute, control. There are four main areas of control: first and foremost the person's own thoughts and feelings, second their own behaviour, third the environment in which they live and finally the people around them. As we shall see later, even the control of God may be on the cards.

Alice lived on her own in a beautifully-designed flat. It looked as if she and the flat had stepped together straight out of a catalogue. Even if she prepared a meal for an occasional visitor, the kitchen surfaces stayed miraculously clean with never a dirty pot in sight. She remained immaculate. Her guests were only ever invited in pairs as she found larger numbers unmanageable. She felt uneasy all the time they were in the flat, could not rest if things were pushed out of place and rushed about repairing the 'damage', rearranging cushions, realigning chairs and so on before they were half-way along the road. Especially, she attended to the bathroom, carefully washing the basin (wearing rubber gloves), changing the towels and disinfecting the loo, before she could begin to relax.

One hidden piece of preparation before anyone came was for Alice to make a list of suitable topics for conversation. This included her writing down actual phrases she would use to start the topic and some anecdotes she could insert if things were not going well during the evening. 'Things not going well' might mean embarrassing subjects like sex or any real difference of opinion arising. This scripting of the evening gave Alice enough sense of control over the other people to keep her own inner feelings, also, under control.

When at the end of the evening it was finally time for bed, Alice went through a strict ritual of closing down the flat for the night. Window locks, doors, switches, lights had to be dealt with in set order. If she was interrupted she had to start again and once she had washed and undressed, again according to a strict ritual, she had to re-check all the locks and switches. Once she was in bed she had to re-run the routine in her mind and, if she felt any doubt, she had to get up and repeat the operation. She sometimes tried to fight the impulse to get up but it was hopeless to resist and she could get no sleep until it was done. Getting to bed was, obviously, an extremely long business, taking her upwards of two hours.

This picture shows Alice to be a woman whose life is quite seriously disturbed by her need to control feelings and events. There are those whose obsessional defences are even more limiting and, of course, there are many, many more people who act obsessionally in milder ways. It is rather a matter of degree.

The degree of tidiness and cleanliness in her flat and her personal appearance go well beyond what is needed for

59

reasonable order and hygiene. It is what a friend of mine used to call 'aggressively clean' so that guests feel hardly free to move and cannot relax. The roots of anxiety for Alice may well be to do with her fears about 'dirty' sex and anything to do with bottoms or toilets sends her for the rubber gloves and disinfectant. These things are the cause of particular anxiety and she has to be on her guard to stop their dangerous influence. We see that in her urgent need to scrub and disinfect as soon as she is alone in the flat again. As long as she feels this is done thoroughly she can relax for a while but if she is going through a particularly stressful time, she may well have to go back and do it again.

This fear that things may not be done properly, that something may have been missed or come undone again, causes Alice and others like her to worry endlessly, to check and re-check that things are as they should be. It is as if the underlying anxiety which they are trying to keep under control is constantly in danger of leaking out like sewage. For some people the anxiety is very strong as if the leak will become a flood which will overwhelm them and they will drown in this filthy chaos. To guard against this, Alice has developed orderly routines for doing things, like locking up for the night. These have a certain sensible and practical logic to them, like the safety routines used by pilots for pre-flight checks, but they are way over the top and, furthermore, need to be re-checked and re-re-checked and even then may fail to satisfy. Sometimes these routines become rituals. They acquire a magic all of their own and, again, may need frequent repetition.

We can see from all this that a person's original attempt to keep anxiety at bay by means of controlling their own feelings and everything around them can backfire alarmingly. The defence becomes so obsessional that *it* ends up controlling them and gives them no peace at all.

In order to live healthily and creatively in society we need a good balance between spontaneous self-expression and control. If our defence against anxiety becomes too strong on the side of control we pay the price in a loss of creativity and spontaneity and make our life so much the poorer. Creativity does not simply mean painting pictures, writing poetry or something similar, it means giving expression to what is inside us, using our imagination, doing something different, playing, letting the spirit move us. The pleasure and joy that is possible in sexual love-making, for example, may be sadly diminished for the man or woman who is trapped in this need for control and, naturally, their partner will also be robbed.

When this kind of obsessional defence is in full swing, it can make life a misery for the person's family as well as for themselves. You can well imagine the lack of freedom a partner and children might feel in a house which must be kept absolutely clean and tidy at all times. Or the frustration and conflict that can arise when one partner must keep a tight control on every penny that is spent in the house. Or the need of someone almost to imprison their partner in the house because of the sexual temptations they fear lurking outside.

A person suffering a lot from this pattern of defence may feel themselves to be on a mental treadmill and in need of professional help such as I talk about in the final chapter.

Compliance

Growing up from early childhood onwards naturally involves adapting our behaviour to fit in more comfortably with our family and society in general. This also involves adopting many of the attitudes, values and beliefs of the people closest to us. When we do this as children, we feel easily accepted by the people we are most dependent on, and so feel secure, a 'good girl' or a 'good boy'; adults smile on us approvingly and all is well with our little world.

Except that all is not well. At least not all the time. Feelings and thoughts get stirred up in us which we know are not approved of. These may arise quite naturally from our childlike urge to play and experiment, like spreading rice pudding through our hair and up the wallpaper, or they may arise in response to something that has been done to us, some parental crossness or neglect which makes us feel angry, jealous or afraid. In any event our safe and comfortable world is disturbed by conflict with those we love. They are angry with us or we with them and this causes a degree of anxiety, perhaps that further punishment will follow or that we will not be allowed back into the security of their love.

What children discover most of the time is that anger and disapproval are not the end of the world and that loving relationships are not broken for ever by one person thinking, feeling and behaving differently from another. Indeed, as we grow we discover that such differences are essential in any genuine relationship. We also discover that we can have very mixed feelings about the same person and that no one is perfectly good. Or, indeed, perfectly bad. We realise this is also true about ourselves. In short, we develop a more mature attitude free from excessive anxiety or defensiveness.

So far so good! But things can take an unhappy turning and rouse such anxiety that the child has to defend him or herself. This may happen because the parents are far too strict and rigid in their attitudes, or too restrictive and prudish, or too punitive. It might be because the whole situation is too insecure, as with parents splitting up or some tragedy striking the family. It might be because the child's emotions are so overpowering. Whatever the cause, the child needs to save the situation and calm his or her awful anxiety. One way of doing this is by becoming overly compliant to what are thought to be the wishes of the parents. The child becomes like Jo.

Jo is 19, an only daughter, though she did have a brother who died when he was 8 and she was only 3. She lives at home with her parents and is very close to them. Her mother is often ill with a variety of conditions which leave her weak and incapable so that it falls on Jo to do much of the domestic work as well as her regular job. Mother is insistent that such jobs are a woman's work and this view is accepted by Jo and her father who does virtually nothing in the house. Practically everything falls on Jo's narrow shoulders. Not that Jo ever complains about the situation. She is well known for her cheerfulness and her willingness to do whatever anyone asks. In fact she finds it so hard to say no to anyone that on one occasion she has ended up having promised two people to baby-sit for them on the same evening. She knew it would be impossible but simply could not bring herself to refuse. As it turned out she had a blinding migraine that night and both people had to be turned down. She felt desperately guilty for days despite repeated reassurances that she was forgiven. Jo has attended church regularly with her parents, without a break, since she was a little girl. She stands out from the other teenagers by dressing in a formal, rather old-fashioned way, and not in jeans and trainers. Her parents take some pride in this though Jo secretly envies her fellow teenagers. Generally, though, she has always got on better with older people. She was very well liked by her teachers at school but never felt in the crowd with the other youngsters. She clearly disapproved of their interest in boys as they grew into their teenage years and they thought her a prude. She was generally ignorant on the matter of sex, a subject never ever mentioned at home. At one time she did have a boyfriend, who was approved of at home as a really nice young man, but she ended the relationship when he tried to get 'too familiar'. She tried to talk to her mother about it but the subject was quickly dropped and has never been mentioned again.

Jo suffers bouts of anxiety depression every so often and even takes to her bed. Though they leave her feeling drained and guilty she works all the harder to catch up on her jobs once the crisis is past.

You see the pattern of compliance clearly in Jo. She has fitted in as far as she is able with the needs and demands of her parents. Although she is nineteen, she is still their little girl, taking up their attitudes to life; doing what is required of her with never a word of complaint. Even when she is taken for granted and made to do almost all the work, there is never a word of protest from her. Not that you should suppose she is feeling put-upon and simply not saying so. Her compliant defence is such that she generally cannot let herself feel any of the angry protest that lies buried inside her. Even the suggestion of it would cause her anxiety.

Anxiety also surrounds the whole realm of sexuality. This has been an area of life which has always caused her mother embarrassment and disgust and this attitude has been passed on to the daughter. Jo complies with this family rule by repressing her own sexual feelings and adopting a prudish attitude. It is also the case that strong sexual feelings in Jo would disturb her by arousing powerful desires and causing her a lot of inner conflict. So all in all it has to be avoided.

Part of her avoidance is by staying clear of her teenage peer group. Whereas most adolescents identify with their peer group as part of growing up and separating from their parents, Jo continues to identify with her mother and father to the extent that she does not develop her own personality.

What we do see in Jo, and in most people who are compliant in this way, is a tendency to feel guilt and occasional periods of depression. (Her mother shows something similar in her frequent spells of illness which are the result of repressed grief.) All the strong feeling of anger, desire and anxiety are held down in such a way that if our defence is working well and we feel approved of by the people who matter to us, and if they seem happy with life, then we are reasonably happy too. But if they seem cross or miserable it can stir up our anxiety and guilt. This is not so much to do with sympathy for their unhappiness as with the belief that their mood is the result of some failure on our part. In the mind of the child, it works like this: 'If I comply with everything they want, they will be pleased with me and love me, and then I will not feel distressed and anxious.' In other words, she controls their mood. If they are unhappy, the child thinks they are unhappy with her and she feels anxious until she can restore things. Of course, the other person's unhappiness may have nothing whatsoever to do with her but this fact may have little or no effect on her feelings.

In her religious life, as you might expect, Jo tries to keep God happy by being as compliant as she knows how. She tries to be the perfect, always willing, always smiling Christian but in reality this is a false front, a false self, behind which is hidden a lot of pain and a sense of injustice which she cannot acknowledge to herself, let alone voice to God or to other people.

The price we pay for this degree of compliance is not only in the bouts of depression or other symptoms we may suffer but in a loss of energy, assertiveness and the freedom to be our God-given self. Feelings of anger and protest, even when they are entirely understandable and justified, may be lost to the extent

64

that authority figures must never be challenged, however incompetent the authority may be. This robs us of the freedom to take adult responsibility for ourselves, to assert what we believe, to make our own decisions and to take initiatives.

In personal relationships, like marriage, such a person may well become a submissive spouse, dominated and exploited by his or her partner. This may suit both parties quite nicely if the defence of both against anxiety is to control everybody around them. The compliance of one may be just what the other is looking for and the other's controlling dominance just what the first wants. But this will be a very sterile relationship which keeps both partners stuck and dissatisfied or, if one begins to grow and spread their wings, this puts a great, if not fatal, strain on the marriage.

We may well begin to wonder why people go on using these and other defences, even unconsciously, when they so impoverish life in the ways I have described: trust, openness, solitude, contentment, intimacy, warmth, meaning, creativity, spontaneity and so forth are all lost or diminished by too high a degree of defensiveness. Even worse than this, people may suffer the painful effects of obsessional behaviour, depression, despair, isolation, etc. when these defences get out of hand or fail in some way.

The extent to which we hang on to our defences is one pointer to the strength of the anxiety in us which the defence has been built to ward off. Secondly, it is a case of 'better the devil you know'. Beginning to relax our defences is to take a risk; we must believe that we will not be flooded by such pain and anxiety that we cannot bear it otherwise we will not, indeed cannot, begin to let the walls down. This requires a degree of trust in the love and support we are able to experience and rely upon in the people around us. For some people such a degree of love and support is found in a religious context, where there are healthy attitudes, faithful to the heart and mind of the Christian gospel. There are also religious attitudes and practices which limit or even run counter to those healing qualities. I shall discuss this in the following two chapters.

6
ANXIETY AND THE CHRISTIAN FAITH

The first thing I want to say on the subject may seem so obvious that it is hardly worth saying at all. However, experience leads me to think that it does need stating clearly and emphatically: Being a Christian does *not* give immunity to anxiety any more than it guarantees freedom from many other forms of human pain and distress. People who have been led to believe that faith in Jesus Christ offers some such guarantee may well become confused and disillusioned when it becomes apparent that this is not the case.

Having said that, does the Christian gospel have within it any understanding about the nature of human existence or any power or resource which can help to allay our deepest anxieties? I believe that it does, and that it is a profound source of strength for our anxious minds. At its most radical it places us in an entirely new set of relationships to God, other people and ourselves so there can be a very real sense of a new life. Given that the roots of our anxiety lie, first and foremost, in basic relationships which were poor or inadequate in some way, the new relationship with God, which is the hallmark of the Christian gospel, provides a new beginning founded on a measure of trust, love and hope.

For the new convert to Christianity, especially if it is a rather sudden conversion, the sense of liberation can be quite overwhelming, like the wonderful feeling of falling in love. All the old worries seem to have disappeared and we feel we have entered a new and brighter world in which we are better, stronger and more vital people. In this new phase of life we may feel that the painful and often damaging experiences of childhood are entirely a thing of the past and that they can and should be totally forgotten. However, again as in falling in love, this early phase is rather idealised, something of a honeymoon period, which sooner or later gives way to a more down to earth form of living, in which the life of faith and love has to be worked out, reaching out to embrace all aspects of human existence. This includes those painful and anxiety-filled experiences of our earlier lives and the hidden parts of ourselves which we feel are unlovable. This is not to say that the honeymoon period, the 'blossom time', as the Danish philosopher Kierkegaard called it, is to be disregarded or devalued on the grounds that it will pass away. It mirrors the earliest experience of the new-born infant held lovingly and securely in the mother's arms which, when it is felt to be good and reliable, forms the basis for gradual growth and individual development which can face up to the harsher realities.

The Christian gospel does not promise long-term freedom from anxiety. That would be to offer people eternal infancy, an existence wrapped in religious cotton wool and the very opposite of the 'abundant life' Jesus talks about. Rather than that, the gospel speaks about human wholeness resulting from learning to face up to the truth, often a very uncomfortable process. In practice this may well mean that far from the Christian faith being a guarantee of freedom from anxiety, or even a reduction in anxiety, in certain ways and at certain times it may lead us into deeper anxiety than we might otherwise experience. On the positive side, however, it should support and contain us in confronting and working through anxiety and living creatively in those situations that give rise to it. Thinking of such situations reminds me of a young man called Paul who became a Christian as an adolescent.

Paul was a 6-year-old evacuee during the Second World War when both his parents were killed in the Blitz. Apparently he showed little reaction when he was told the news, he did not want to talk about it and nobody gave him any encouragement to do so. When he looked back on those days years later he said that the loss of his parents seemed to make little impact on him. After the war he returned to London where he lived with his grandma. At 14 he was expelled from school for persistent misbehaviour and later he was in and out of work. Twice he was in trouble with the police for minor offences whilst drunk.

Underneath a tough and uncaring exterior, Paul felt a mixture of gloom and unhappiness on the one hand and on the other, periods of quite murderous rage. It was this latter feeling which indirectly led to his conversion to Christianity.

One day he got into an argument with another lad when he had had a few drinks, attacking him so violently that he had to be hospitalised. This so affected him that he became afraid in a way that he had never been before and for the first time he began to talk to another resident in his hostel. This man, a young Christian, formed a friendship with Paul which became instrumental in his conversion to Christianity. As you might expect, he was quite dramatically changed by this experience. In the church he found a family atmosphere such as he could never remember in his whole life before, he felt forgiven and accepted and very much at peace with God. He got involved in the church and began to study for a fresh start.

It was when his plans hit a snag that Paul realised his 'old-self' as he often called it, was not as totally extinct as he had thought. He faced this unavoidable fact when he could not find a college place to pursue what he had come to believe was God's plan for him. He felt overwhelmed by frightening fantasies of destroying the church and attacking God by whom he felt totally betrayed. After a few days, these feelings gave way to a terrible anxiety in which he felt he was falling apart and that he had lost everything he had come to believe in. He tried to go on as if nothing had happened but gradually he let it all come out: at first about the recent crisis of faith, then into the deeper waters of his long-buried past and all the rage, terror and grief associated with his evacuation and the tragedy of his parents' death.

The outcome of all this was not that Paul was 'cured' of these feelings so that he never felt anxiety or anger again; neither was it that he returned to the rather magical days following his conversion. But it did mean that he became a more whole person, noticeably more tolerant and compassionate than he had been, not only in the days before his conversion, but in the proud days following it.

The story of Paul, admittedly a rather dramatic one, does illustrate well a common Christian experience: at first we may find the gospel allays many old fears and doubts but later the spiritual life causes us to face, perhaps, deeper anxieties which have been a long time hidden in the unconscious mind. In Paul's case the childhood catastrophe of losing his parents so violently and when he had so little support aroused such dreadful anxiety in his young mind that simply to survive emotionally he had to dam it up so that it would not overwhelm him. He survived for years by aggressively withdrawing from the world around him. Only when he felt the safety his new faith gave him was he able to begin the painful task of embracing the terrified and raging little boy inside him.

In many ways we are challenged by the gospel to recognise and discard our masks and defences by faith in the goodness of God. This is often an anxious process. Put in the language of the Christian faith, it is losing one's life in order to find it, it is dying to be reborn, it is facing weakness to experience God's strength. Confidence to open ourselves to this process depends on trust in the loving nature and goodness of God. It also depends on what we believe about our nature as human beings. Let us look at this more closely.

People, Good or Bad?

The other day I heard two men from the church arguing about the basic nature of humankind: one said he believed that people were basically bad, the other countered that they were basically good. Each thought that the Christian faith supported his point of view. This does seem a most important question because if we believe that the most basic truth about ourselves is that we are bad, that is to say destructive, ugly and hateful, it seems fair to assume that we need to be strongly controlled from doing harm by various means. It also means that to reveal too much of what is inside us, hidden away in our secret mind and feelings, is to be avoided at all costs for fear that if it comes to light it will result in rejection, punishment and death. Indeed this is just how some people do feel about themselves. They live in constant anxiety that their bad self will break out and broadcast their awfulness to everyone they know. Perhaps they see their anxiety as a useful warning to reinforce their repressive defences, and they may treat religion as a policeman to keep them in order. If on the other hand we believe that our basic nature is good, that is to say creative, beautiful and loving, then the job of getting in touch with that true, good self and encouraging it to grow and flower is a worthwhile aim in life. Anxious defences may then be seen as useful to survival when we are fragile and endangered but ultimately as life-denying and needing, with God's help, to be overcome.

The Christian gospel, with its roots in the Old Testament, has two beliefs about the nature of humankind which are basic. The first of these is that people are created in God's image. As Genesis 1.27 puts it, 'God created man [i.e. human beings] in his own image; in the image of God he created him; male and female he created them.' The second is that we have a fundamental need to be in a positive, loving relationship with God, other people and ourselves. Jesus states this as the summary of the Jewish law and goes as far as to say that it is so basic that everything else rests on this fact. It is recorded in Matthew 22.37 in these words:

> Love the Lord your God with all your heart, with all your soul and with all your mind. That is the greatest commandment. It comes first. The second is like it: Love your neighbour as yourself. Everything in the law and the prophets hangs on these two commandments.

Both say things which are important to every person and not least to those who are insecure about who they are and fear that their true and hidden self is so frightful and unacceptable that it must continue to be hidden away.

In saying that men and women are made in the image of God, Jewish and Christian religion rests on the view that people are basically good, that is, have the ability to love and to create, to want justice and to show mercy and compassion, those being among the most fundamental qualities of God.

But what about the dreadful things we do to each other which are so apparent in the world around us? What about oppression, neglect, injustice and cruelty? How do they fit into a view of humanity as 'basically good'? That is a most important question and to go into it thoroughly is well beyond the scope of this book. Nevertheless I want to make certain points.

First, the Jewish/Christian tradition and teaching in no way ignores the problem of badness and destruction in humanity and the world at large even though it begins with the picture of a good creation. It sees that fundamental goodness as having been spoilt but it also holds on to a belief in the greater power of goodness to outlast and overcome badness.

Second, the capacity for cruelty and every kind of destructiveness is in every one of us and we need to face it and come to terms with it if we want to limit its more subtle influences. This is a question of spiritual development which is a lifetime's work. At the risk of repeating myself, let me say again that the process of coming to terms with our inner reality may cause more, rather than less, anxiety on the way.

Third, for some people who have grown up in an atmosphere of insecurity and endless criticism so that they felt they could never get it right, they are convinced only of their badness and need to be encouraged to accept and trust the essential goodness which God sees in them even if it is presently hidden from themselves. They may be people who avoid letting anyone get too close to them for fear of rejection or judgement and, in doing this, make their situation even worse by denying themselves the intimate love which they desperately need.

Good Relations

This brings me to the second of the two beliefs about the nature of humankind. That is that we need to be in good relationships, relationships of love with God, other people and ourselves. As I have said in a variety of ways already, many people who suffer the more disabling kinds of anxiety do so because their early relationships were not good enough to build them up in confidence and security. They may be people who have turned away from others because their trust has been so dented and they have suffered so deeply that they are determined to avoid the same thing happening again. They may be looking for satisfaction in other ways but fail to find it exactly because these ways are a substitute for their more basic need. This need is not fulfilled by casual or shallow relationships, though the way we live will inevitably involve a tremendous number of these, many of which will be delightful and enriching. The more basic need is for some experience of intimacy in which we encounter another person in a deep and unguarded way and know that we are known.

Christianity is above all a religion of relationships which uses the language of relationships to describe its most important ideas and beliefs: God is described as a loving parent, the relationship between Christ and the church as that between a husband and wife, the great virtues are personal: kindness, patience, forgiveness, faithfulness and so on; the new commandment which Jesus gives his followers is inter-personal, that they should love one another (John 13.34). Most central of all is the Christian belief that Christ's mission was nothing if not to do with a relationship, that between God and you and me which needs to be repaired when it is broken down.

This focus on good, loving and intimate relationships both as a philosophy and a way of life is a tremendous resource (in religious terms a means of grace) for any of us suffering anxiety. That is to say, it is a tremendous resource when it is preached and practised well and according to a whole and healthy balance of the gospel. However it can and, regrettably, too often is practised in such ways that its helpfulness is limited or, more seriously, it is actually harmful and causes more anxiety, guilt and depression than it relieves.

I will explain in more detail what I think are the basic and most helpful characteristics of Christian belief for the over anxious person, and then go on to describe what I think are unhealthy and unhelpful attitudes. Naturally what is unhelpful for the more anxious among us is also unhelpful for the less anxious, but these are probably less vulnerable people and can cope more robustly with mistakes.

Unconditional Acceptance

First among positive characteristics is the Christian belief that God accepts us in an unconditional way. (This assumes that the church behaves in the kind of way that demonstrates God's acceptance.) Of course, unconditional does not mean that God is indifferent to how we think, feel and behave, but it does mean that there are no pre-conditions to the relationship. This is similar to the way in which a baby needs to be accepted by his or her parents when newly born, not merely accepted on the basis of being 'the right sex' or having this or that particular feature, but simply on the basis of being a living human being. In the case of God, acceptance of us goes further because we believe God is fully aware of the still hidden parts of us, with all that we feel ashamed or bad about, all that we dread coming to light. All this is accepted as part and parcel of who we are. Indeed God's acceptance goes even further because we believe he knows the most secret parts of our inner world which we have so far kept hidden even from ourselves, and these are all embraced. This includes all the positive and creative potential but also what is sometimes called the dark or shadow side of us. If we know and can begin to believe that we are acceptable even to those depths of ourselves, and that we are not punished or killed off because we are too awful to exist, then our anxiety may begin to lose some of its power and loosen its stranglehold on us.

The power of such acceptance will depend to a great extent on how successfully the church can reflect that tremendous quality of God. It cannot and need not reflect it perfectly but it must do so to an adequate degree if people coming in to it are to experience acceptance and not only have it preached to them as a theory. I remember one man in a counselling group saying, 'I've been a Christian for years and years and have heard all about love and acceptance but this is the first time I've actually experienced it.'

Security

Second on my list is the security that Christianity offers. This is firstly the security of the relationship of acceptance I have just spoken about, but it is more than that. Christianity gives a framework of belief to help us make sense of the world and our place in it, it gives us a sense of meaning which is able to combat the dreadful sense of meaninglessness which lies at the heart of much anxiety. In saying this I am not suggesting that Christianity provides a neat and watertight set of answers to all the questions our lives might bring up, but it gives a framework of belief to hold and contain us when we are like dependent and vulnerable children who need to be held in a secure embrace. And for us as adults, it is something like a set of maps and signposts when we are making our journey through life: through youth and adulthood towards old age and eventual death.

This journey will take us into some dark places, into the dark night of the soul, as St John of the Cross called it, and there our anxiety may be intense like Graham's (see p. 23). There may also be strong feelings of doubt and despair which go along with the anxiety. The support of the church can be vital here, helping to put into words and into the framework of faith an experience that can be so desperately disturbing to the sufferer. It can also encourage the fragile flame of faith and hope to stay alive.

Confrontation

The next positive quality is that the Christian faith confronts and challenges us. At first sight this may seem unhelpful if we are suffering from anxiety and need support and acceptance. However, it is not only helpful, it is necessary for there to be a degree of confrontation if there is to be growth and development. This is self-evident in the development of children from infancy onwards who become spoilt if they have all their short-term needs met without experiencing frustration or challenge. The need for confrontation is also well recognised in the business of counselling and psychotherapy. People do need a lot of support and understanding, but they also need someone to help them face the often uncomfortable truth about themselves and the world around them if they are to improve and come to terms with their difficulties.

St Paul mentions such confrontation in his phrase 'speaking the truth in love'. It needs to be a feature of the church's life which is very sensitively handled if it is to be effective. We have to beware of the self-appointed guardians of other people's lives who want to control everybody else under the cover of doing the Lord's work. Such people are found in church congregations as well as in other spheres of life. We have to be equally wary of the sadistic tendencies lurking in all of us which are capable of punishing with 'the truth'. But having said that, some degree of confrontation is provided by the week in, week out life of a healthy congregation and additional specific confrontation which also supports and encourages the anxious person can be very positive. Perhaps an example will be helpful here in showing what I mean.

Sarah lived a rather withdrawn life; she also suffered a great deal of anxiety, which she kept secret from other people, and had a low opinion of her own worth. She attended the local church but kept people at a distance. This particular church suited her rather well: people were friendly but in a rather distant sort of way. She was able to come and go and felt more and more comfortable about being accepted; she was able to listen to the excellent teaching so that her views about herself and the world changed quite radically. Nevertheless she remained untouched in certain important respects. It was as if her feelings and emotions were in a separate compartment and did not change. She remained deeply isolated and there was nothing in the life of the church which challenged this.

After a couple of years a new vicar came and began to make a few changes to the services. They included a new practice which involved people holding each other's hands and saying, 'Peace be with you'. Most of the congregation seemed to take to it after a little embarrassment but Sarah was filled with a degree of horror she could not understand. She felt trapped and desperately anxious, so much so that she simply could not face going to church. When the vicar visited she gave a number of excuses for her absence. None of them seemed genuine to him though the vicar did wonder if it would be best to take them at face value. He felt pretty confident that her relationship with him was basically sound so he told her that he wondered if she was running away from something. She reacted angrily and said that he had spoilt things for her: the 'peace' was no peace any more for her, and she was furious about it. He said he was sorry.

Sarah was silent for a while, then said that she did not know why she reacted so strongly. She was quiet again, then began to say how afraid she felt whenever anyone came near her physically and especially when they touched her. She thought she had always felt this way as long as she could remember.

All this proved to be a critical moment for the young woman confronted by these deep fears which for years had kept her isolated from other people and from her own need to love and be loved. Her problems were by no means instantly resolved, as what began to come to light was a history of physical abuse and neglect which had caused her to withdraw further and further from other people and deeper into nearly total mistrust. She found support in the simple acceptance of her in the local church and in her growing belief that she could trust the church not to let her down or turn against her. She was able to get professional help to work through much of the pain which had resulted from her childhood. Gradually she was able to confront the physical fear about being touched and to be generally more open both in receiving and giving to other people once her anxiety had begun to be confronted by the threat of intimacy.

Fellowship

The fourth positive quality I want to mention has already been touched on in the example I just gave: a fellowship of people who are genuine, open and honest with each other but at the same time respect the rights of other people to be private and to be separate individuals. Because of the high ideals of Christianity, there can be quite a strong temptation in the church for people to put on a mask of some kind and not let other people see what is the true person underneath. This is, of course, the very opposite of what the Christian faith is about. Jesus confronted people who were like this very strongly. Among other things he called them 'whitewashed tombs'. In such an atmosphere you begin to feel like a performer acting a part with the constant anxiety that you will forget your lines. On the other hand I have known Christian fellowships which have gone so far overboard in their attempts to be absolutely open and honest that they have developed a new kind of tyranny in which people feel invaded and exposed. This can do a great deal of harm and in some cases push the very anxious person right over the edge into a state of panic.

So the best atmosphere is one in which people are real and open whilst at the same time respecting other people's God-given right to be who they are; to have their own thoughts and feelings respected. We need people to be warm and caring without taking us over either in the sense of being like a warm and too deep bath in which we are at risk of drowning, sometimes called smother-love, or in the sense of telling us what to think and forcing their beliefs on us like dominant parents. In a practical sense the kind of relationships of openness and respect which I am trying to describe are often best achieved in the life of a local church within a house-group or some similar small grouping which can allow trust to develop and let people feel safe enough to share themselves honestly and speak about some of their anxieties while being supported in the love of other people.

Having said that, the mere existence of such small groups is no guarantee of their being used to foster openness and trust. The little 'Führer' unwisely appointed to lead such a group, for example, can cause a great deal of distress. On the other hand, leaders who are sensitive and not defensively anxious themselves can prove invaluable. Of course, they need to recognise the limits of their ability to help. In practice that may mean knowing who they can talk to if they feel things are beyond them.

Worship and Ritual

The most obvious way the church works is by meeting for its services of worship and the question arises about whether these occasions can be a positive help to people who are anxious. I know that for some people churches are strange and rather forbidding places and more likely to provoke anxiety than to relieve it. On the other hand, for people who become familiar with the place and what goes on inside it, who have some belief in what it stands for, the regular patterns of worship and prayer provide a valuable and secure framework.

Churches vary greatly in the way they conduct their services: some use a lot of ritual which is acted out in dramatic ways, others use rather more words and rather less action, some are quiet and restrained, others loud and flamboyant. This book does not allow the space to go into the nature of these differences in much detail, but it is enough to say for the moment that each in its own way provides a kind of language of communication between God and people. In this sense, both spoken and written words, as well as sounds, pictures, actions, colours and so forth, are symbols, outward signs of inward realities. The important point I want to make is that such worship takes us as isolated, vulnerable and anxious individuals, often feeling lost or power-less in the face of universal issues or so caught in our self-centred concerns that we are in danger of losing all perspective; it places us, symbolically, in a right relationship to God, other people, the created order and, last but not least, ourselves. That is to say, it is a dramatic way of representing the great commandment to love God and your neighbour as yourself.

Christians believe that the relationship of acceptance, truth and love with God, which is symbolically re-enacted in worship, touches our deepest human need for fulfilment and satisfaction. For the moment the potential peace and beauty of that relation-ship may be hidden underneath all sorts of fear and anxiety and beneath the layers of defensiveness we have built against abuse and neglect earlier in life. Our anxieties are not magicked away by our becoming Christians. Particularly if we have been very hurt by life experiences, our faith in God's goodness and trust-worthiness may be very fragile at times but the rituals and life of the church offer a way of affirming and reaffirming our faith and hope in that relationship as something which is coming about. At its most effective the church is able to contain us with our anxieties and help us to grow. At times when we have become too distressed, like Sarah in my earlier example, we may need additional and more specialised help. This will be the subject of the final chapter.

7
UNHELPFUL RELIGIOUS ATTITUDES

All that I have said so far about the help that the normal life of the church can give anxious people paints a very positive picture indeed. I wish that it were the case that the church always followed good and healthy practices that could both contain us with our distress and help us to grow so that we become freer, less anxious and generally more whole. But the reality is that there are some ways in which religion is practised which either contain people with their anxieties without going on to help them develop or (and this is much worse) actually provoke them into greater anxiety or leave them feeling trapped and oppressed. We need the church to be like a good family which supports and feeds its children properly according to their stage of development but which does not keep them needlessly in over-anxious dependency. When anxious children have to move on a stage, like starting school or leaving home, or have to deal with difficulties like bullying or making and losing relationships, they need support and encouragement but not blaming or over-protection.

Of course, to avoid anxiety, many, including adults, may dream of remaining as little children in the never-ending protection of mummy and daddy, but wise parents will not collude with this for ever. They know it will emotionally and spiritually impoverish the lives of their offspring. Unfortunately, some parents who, for their own emotional needs, wish to keep their children eternally dependent on them, go further than mere collusion by encouraging or even imposing anxiety on them.

The church can easily fall into such ways of behaving, being like well-intentioned but ultimately unhelpful parents who collude with neurotic defences against the uncertainties and responsibilities of life, or actually encourage anxiety and guilt to reinforce dependence. Instead of faith being a means of growth into fuller maturity and freedom it can prop up an already neurotic way of living.

In this chapter I want to talk about several ways in which this can happen. Each is a type of religious attitude or practice that is attractive to some people but each has a negative side to it which, in terms of dealing with anxiety, is ultimately unhelpful. I will call these types of religion: 'Oughtism', Fundamentalism, Triumphalism, Intellectualism and Obsessionalism.

As you will see, I am not talking about whole denominations, but it will be obvious to some readers who know their way around the church that some denominations are more prone to certain negative qualities than others. My own church, the Church of England, has a share of them all in different places. Of course, every local church will exhibit all or most of these qualities to some degree just as every person will show negative as well as positive characteristics. In moderation each quality can be of help to people at certain times in their lives. However, my concern is where these qualities are dominant in the life and practice of a particular church to the extent that people who suffer particularly badly from anxiety are not well served. I will talk about each type in turn.

'Oughtism'

This is a 'big brother is watching you' kind of religion. It is dominated by what psychoanalysts might call the super-ego or the critical parent. That is the part of the psyche which tells us what we 'ought' and 'ought not' to do, hence the term 'oughtism', and hints at or even openly threatens with terrible consequences if we do not obey. Although everybody, by the very fact of being brought up by parental figures of one sort or another, is conditioned to behave in certain ways which are acceptable and to avoid other, unacceptable ways of behaving, some people are very heavily oppressed by these internal demands, as I described in Chapter 5, and are likely to become both anxious and depressed if they go against them.

Such people tend to hear criticism of themselves even when it is not intended and are for ever saying they are sorry when there is no apparent reason. They live with a permanent feeling that they cannot get it right or come up to the required standard, even when people around them are not putting pressure on them. Imagine how vulnerable such people are under the authority of a church or pastor who is like a dominant parent telling people how they must behave, using the authority of the church or scripture to justify this over-zealous behaviour and making, or at least implying, dire threats if there is disobedience.

Such religious practice usually emphasises the bad and sinful nature of humankind and the message is clearly that people deserve to be punished and that feeling bad about yourself is appropriate. Although their creed speaks of grace and forgiveness, what they really live by is massive guilt and hard work. Let me unwrap that. A church may teach that people are brought into a good relationship with God because God is merciful and forgiving and loves people; the relationship does not depend on people earning their acceptance and forgiveness by trying harder and harder to be perfectly obedient. Nevertheless the ministers and pastors continue to emphasise failure and play on people's guilt as a way of controlling them. It is like a parent saying to an already insecure child, 'If you are not a good girl, daddy won't love you any more.' This is where 'good' means 'obey unquestioningly what I tell you'.

In my experience, such religion is particularly repressive of two things: sex and aggression. Both these powerful forces, which are so central to our human nature, are things we have to come to terms with in the process of growing up and, as children and later as adolescents, we need an environment which is secure in order to do that. Very controlling and repressive parents or those who are over anxious about their own aggressive or sexual feelings do not create such an environment. The person grows up profoundly uneasy about these troublesome forces within, terribly guilty about masturbation for example, terribly guilty about feeling angry or ever standing up for themselves however badly used they may be. They are vulnerable to the kind of religion which will play on their anxiety and guilt, effectively keeping them stuck and preventing them from experiencing the freedom the Christian gospel promises, but in this case denies.

In the first instance, people who are troubled by strong personal oughtism and live under a cloud of neurotic guilt and anxiety are attracted by this kind of religious emphasis, especially as adolescents, when the church offers to take on the role of the controlling parent, promising God's eternal love, if they are obedient, and generally assuming responsibility for them. At the same time they are told, and continue to be told, what miserable sinners they are (which their super-ego has already done all their lives). Initially this helps them to feel secure and free from anxiety. It acts as a further layer to their psychological defences to anxiety and provides regular doses of teaching to give further reinforcement to the message of conditional rather than unconditional love.

I think that in many cases a rather parental type of church serves a useful purpose and provides a helpful stage for those who need such security at a vulnerable time in their lives. For example young people going away from home for the first time to college or university seem often to be drawn to this kind of religion and it is for them a stage of transition. But problems arise when the leaders of the church, because of their own personalities, continue to exercise a strong super-ego influence, making God's love conditional and punitive, and continuing to repress what is judged unacceptable. This is not necessarily done in a harsh or cynical way, but people can be powerfully manipulated. The less anxious will grow through this to a more mature faith, but others may leave the church disillusioned. The more anxious may need help to break away or else may remain stuck.

Fundamentalism

I am using the term fundamentalism here not simply to refer to people who are biblical fundamentalists (that is those who understand the Bible in a word for word literal sense), but to refer to any kind of Christian group which offers one narrow way of understanding experience and rules out all those people who do not share their beliefs. This sort of religion offers people a lot of security and a strong group identity. If you belong you know exactly who your friends are and, equally importantly, who your enemies are. You know exactly what you are required to believe and what you must do. Clearly this is a tempting proposition to some over anxious people who feel all at sea in a world of uncertainty and relative values.

Fundamentalism is above all an attempt to gain a totally predictable world. It is a bid to counter anxiety in a world where, at a human level, the only certainty seems to be one's eventual physical death. Christianity does not deal in certainty but in a relationship of faith and this is a very different thing. Fundamentalism wants to tie God down, to make God predictable and controllable. What it succeeds in doing is tying its adherents down. Fundamentalism offers security but it is the security provided by a prison with thick walls enclosing a narrow space.

For many who have grown up as children in a rigid and controlling family, adolescence and young adulthood often bring considerable anxiety as they engage more and more with the complexities of the real, grown-up world. They may restrict their involvement as far as possible by working and socialising within the group of believers and this may succeed in reducing conflict and keeping anxiety within reasonable bounds. For others anxiety becomes intense, they want to break out, yet feel an almost intolerable anxiety when they attempt to do so. They feel angry about being trapped but fearful about opposing the rules that their fundamentalism lays down, fearful of crossing over the line that has always separated them from those outside the elect. This conflict often produces depression as well as anxiety and they can feel so totally trapped within this irreconcilable conflict that they despair and become suicidal. This situation is so intense because it does not only involve disobedience of their parents but of a God who they fear will condemn them to everlasting damnation.

One of the ways such groups protect themselves against the influence of others is by saying that anyone who criticises or questions them is 'of the devil' and 'Satan trying to lead them astray'. This means that any person who seriously questions them must be totally rejected including, of course, other Christians who criticise them. This can make it very difficult for people who feel anxiously trapped to trust their own feelings or the encouragement of a counsellor from outside the group of believers to examine openly and honestly what is happening to them. In practice, I am glad to say, people do find the courage and strength to oppose the life-denying aspects of such fundamentalism by facing their anxieties within a supportive relationship.

Alec grew up with a narrow, fundamentalist background. His father was the pastor of their church. From early in his life, Alec always felt at home there. Indeed he felt more comfortable than at home because his father was predictably good-humoured there. At school the boy was rather isolated as he was under instructions from home not to make friends among his classmates. It never really occurred to him to challenge his parents over this, having grown up with the belief that most people outside their fellowship were a bad influence. For the most part his parents were pleased with him but, inevitably, there were times when he did upset them by some minor disobedience. Then his father would punish him suddenly and without explanation. The punishments were harsh and humiliating and Alec was left feeling that, by his failure to walk the narrow path, he had deeply wounded both his father and God who, not surprisingly, were one and the same in his mind.

As he began to mature sexually Alec had times of growing anxiety. He was too isolated from his peers at school to join in the talk about sex, what was preached in the church seemed to him firmly against it and he was too afraid to speak to his parents for fear it might trigger one of his father's terrifying outbursts. He withdrew further into isolation.

At 18 when he went to Bible college, he was intensely distrustful and anxious about leaving the narrow security of home but despite this, he became involved in the college fellowship which, whilst still biblically focused, was much, much freer than the church back home. His pastoral tutor was a sensitive and caring man who challenged any of the students who became too exclusive or judgemental, and Alec slowly began to develop some trust in him, to think for himself and then to voice some doubts about the strict faith he had inherited. In short, he began to loosen the yoke his father had laid on him. It made him nervous to do it but he felt he should write to his father and tell him what was happening.

He received a reply and they agreed to talk in the holidays but, before they could meet, his father had a severe heart attack. He survived it but Alec collapsed into an acute anxiety depression convinced that he had caused his father's near death by daring to challenge what he had been taught. He feared that if he persisted in his disobedience he would surely kill him.

At this stage Alec could easily have let his anxiety drive him back into the safety of his father's fundamentalism but with the encouragement of his pastor and the help of a counsellor he continued his struggle towards greater freedom and trust in a God who would not destroy him for being the man God had created. Eventually he was able to master his anxiety enough to talk to his father, but only after he had faced up to his enormous rage at him for his harsh injustice.

Triumphalism

Triumphalism produces another lopsided version of Christianity which is seductive to many people who suffer anxiety, but which does them no favours in the long run.

An important part of Christianity is a belief in the victorious outcome of the power of love, goodness and creativity over the power of hatred, evil and destruction and the belief that this has been achieved through the person of Jesus Christ. And we further believe, in terms of time and eternity, that this victory has both been achieved and *is being achieved*. That it is being achieved means that it is being worked out in the experience of us all and, of course, this means that we have to go through times which are painful, confusing and frightening as we journey on.

However, there are those groups in the church which want to put the whole focus of Christianity on the victorious aspect of the gospel, whilst virtually ignoring the parts which are hard and painful to take on. They want to stress those parts of Christian worship which are to do with praise and joy almost to the exclusion of everything else. The group pressure to express only positive feelings of joy, hope and praise can be so great that people are sometimes accused of lack of faith when they say they are feeling afraid, depressed, even sad. I have come across situations where bereaved people have been persuaded by such pressure to deny their feelings of grief, for example, and feel they should only be joyful that a loved one, a husband, wife or even child, has died and 'gone to be with the Lord'. This sort of religious pressure is a denial of our God-given humanity and ignores much of the very human picture of Jesus which is given in the gospels which includes his grief and distress.

Of course, loss, bereavement and the certainty of our own death are all things which rouse deep anxieties in us and for this reason there is a part of every one of us that wants to ignore these dark thoughts and fears and think happy thoughts. But the Christian church is the last place where death and suffering should be ignored. The church does have a language to speak about death and has its rituals and pastoral care to help hold people in their grief and fear. Sadly, though, there are triumphalistic churches which pretty much deny the reality of pain and darkness in the spiritual life, not only in regard to loss and bereavement but in regard to the whole process of people coming to terms with the shadow side of life.

When people are encouraged or even pressured into denying the dark and painful part of their experience and are led to believe that even feeling such pain is a betrayal of their faith, they are pushed deeper and deeper into their underlying anxiety and become more and more cut off from their true selves. Eventually they pay the price for this denial in some kind of emotional breakdown, depression or despair which may be much more severe than the original trauma. If they are still dependent for their support on the ministry of a very triumphalistic church they may find themselves effectively rejected. isolated and blamed for their sorry state.

During the years in which I worked at one or other of the Church Army's counselling centres, we regularly had people coming to us who were members of certain rather triumphalistic churches. They had a variety of problems along with one that was common to them all: they felt sure that they could not begin to speak about their negative feelings and fears within the fellowship of their churches, even though they were members of supposedly close, supportive groups, without being condemned for lack of faith in a way that added depression to their other problems. Of course, part of the picture was that they were condemning themselves for their supposed failure, but that condemnation was roundly supported by others who felt they were somehow letting the side down and spoiling the joyfulness of it all. They felt, possibly accurately, that people wanted to get rid of them in much the same way as you might be glad when a miserable person leaves a party.

Intellectualism

As with the other rather lopsided versions of Christianity I have mentioned, this can be a way of helping some people to contain their anxiety in a secure framework. From that point of view it is very appealing, though again, in its more extreme forms it is limiting. It values ideas, not only above everything else, but to the extent that other ways of understanding, through intuition and feeling for example, are looked down on.

At first sight this kind of religion may seem more benign than some of the others in this chapter as it is not so militant about converting other people to its point of view. The over anxious may not seem so vulnerable to its attitudes. Nevertheless it is capable of breeding a superiority which can be quite contemptuous of other people, reinforcing in some a sense of uneasy inferiority.

Some very anxious people try to deal with their anxiety by not thinking about things realistically. Religion becomes, for them, a way of escape from the world, as in the triumphalism I have just talked about. However, some others escape from the world, especially the world of relationships and emotion and the anxiety this causes them, by retreating into rational explanations for everything. This becomes a substitute for the human need to relate. As Christians, to quote an old phrase, they have God in the head but not in the heart.

Of course we must use our intelligence about religious and moral issues, and try to understand the life of faith and make sense of the complex world in which we live. But like all good things the intellect can go too far when it excludes other ways of understanding and engaging with God and the world. If we find this aspect of religion very comfortable and gain a sense of security and intellectual pleasure from it, an attitude of detached superiority can easily grow. At its worst this may become a feeling of actual contempt for much of humanity. This can be hurtful and damaging to other people as well as to ourselves.

The down side of it may also be that we are rather isolated; that we may experience an inner hunger which we are unable to satisfy and which our religion fails to meet. Perhaps partly we long to let ourselves go and risk experiencing other more expressive and involved ways of worship and fellowship but even to think about it, let alone do it, arouses our anxiety so we retreat into our intellectual detachment. Perhaps there are some risks we could take within the life of our church, or somewhere else, to get a bit closer to other people and more involved in non-intellectual things, but we fearfully hold back.

Obsessionalism

The last of these five types of religion which can be unhelpful and not altogether healthy is the obsessional one. As I have already said in earlier chapters, obsessional behaviour is one way of trying to keep control of anxiety by various 'rituals' which the person has to perform again and again in order to feel safe and to manage life. If they fail to do exactly what the ritual demands they cannot cope and become overwhelmed by anxiety. Some religious practices take on this obsessional flavour.

Christian practice makes use of many rituals as symbolic ways of picturing and speaking about inner spiritual truths. They are outward expressions of the relationship between God and people. But sometimes these rituals seem to get hijacked by obsessional people who rather distort them. What I mean is that they become powerful, magical ways of doing things to ward off bad and anxious feelings. The power of God's love becomes displaced by the power of the ritual itself. To put it another way, God becomes magically controlled by the use of the ritual so that faith is in the correct performance of the ritual rather than in the person of God. Of course, even if people behave in this way, they will not say that this is what they believe is happening, but such religious practice suggests that this is what is really and truly believed.

What tends to give the game away is firstly that the ritual must be performed with absolute and exact precision and must always be done in exactly the same way. For example things being set out for worship must be placed precisely in the 'right' place, not a centimetre to the left or to the right, and must be done in the inflexibly correct order. Words and actions must be according to a certain formula and tradition. Second, when things are not done precisely and correctly and people deviate, they or other people in the church feel a rush of anxiety, alarm or anger out of all proportion to the situation. Newcomers to the church must be regimented into the right way of doing things and in the extreme this can become quite persecutory. Some years ago I stayed for a short while in a theological college where this sort of thing had got right out of hand. For the most part the worshippers in the chapel spoke and acted with such automatic precision and regimentation that a drill sergeant from the brigade of guards would not have been disappointed had he made a visit. The more sinister aspect of the situation was that individuals spoke to me personally about how persecuted they had felt by a number of other students when they had done something differently in their first year.

I am not suggesting that such extremes are common or that orderliness is a bad thing. Ritual and discipline in worship can be very helpful, not least to the over anxious person, when it is kept within reasonable bounds. But it is worth remembering that for the obsessional person, their obsessions and rituals can become a nightmare, 'torture' as one person said to me recently. They help to ward off anxiety when they are precisely obeyed but tend to become more and more demanding and place strict limits on the person's freedom. If the church is in the hands of leaders who are very controlling of other people and the whole life of the church centres around rather obsessional rituals which are pressed upon people, the whole thing may further trap those it is supposed to set free and create more anxiety than it relieves.

Where does all this leave us?

In Chapters 6 and 7 I have tried to do two things: to say what I think are some of the strengths of Christianity when it is taught and practised in the best traditions of the church (that is in ways which will greatly help us with our over-anxious lives); and to look at ways in which religion is distorted by taking some part of the whole which is basically good and blowing it up out of proportion.

As far as over-anxiety is concerned, I believe that a healthy religion will do, again, two things: it will help to contain and hold us with our anxiety, and it will help us towards greater freedom from the negative affects of the anxiety. In the practices of religion I have criticised as unhelpful, there is a failure in the second of those things and sometimes even in the first.

If you are a Christian and a member of a church you may well be comparing yourself and your church with the religious attitudes I have described. I hope you will bear in mind that no church, any more than any person, is perfect and that most churches will tend to be stronger in some respects than in others. Also remember that different personalities are very positively helped by different styles and approaches to the same gospel. This is a great strength of Christianity. I am only concerned about those churches which take certain aspects of religion to an extreme and in doing that load more anxiety and guilt on already anxious and guilty people or keep people safe but dependent. If you are a Christian and a church-goer, how do you find things? You may often be asked how you are serving the church. How is the church serving you?

8
LIVING WITH ANXIETY

In Chapter 6 I talked about some of the ways in which the Christian gospel and life within the Christian community can prove a source of support and encouragement to anxious people. In this chapter I want to think more generally about some of the ways in which you can manage to cope with your own anxiety, both with and without the help of close relatives and friends. In the final chapter I will go on to outline what professional help is available if you suffer anxiety or panic attacks for which you want further help. It may be you are someone for whom anxiety is an ongoing problem, whether mild or more severe, or someone who is suffering a period of unusually intense anxiety because of a particular situation. Even if you decide to seek professional help, what I have to say in this chapter should prove relevant, though, of course, not everything will be helpful to everyone. You may want to experiment to find your own best way of managing it. Remember that I am not talking here about curing anxiety, though you may find that as you manage it better you suffer it less in the sense that you are not so anxious about being anxious.

Attitude

As with much else in life, so with anxiety, our basic attitude is a large part of the problem, and changing that attitude is half the battle. If you tend to believe that fear and anxiety are always signs of weakness and that you should never feel apprehensive, let alone terrified, you will find it impossible to accept your true feelings and come to terms with them. You may then tend to deny that you are ever anxious, not only to other people, but to yourself. The need to survive in an emotionally or physically desperate situation may cause a repression of fear and anxiety which may be temporary or become habitual. As I have already commented, many men in British culture have been conditioned to believe that they should never show fear, never cry and always be brave. More than a few women have been raised with the same expectation. This attitude is not without its value in some circumstances where fear may be disabling and aggression more useful. For example, if a society wants to breed warriors to fight its battles it has an interest in conditioning the small boys it produces to repress their fear and anxiety and develop more angry responses as they grow to manhood. Over the years mothers as well as fathers have played a key role in this conditioning. As modern life has developed and the more pressing need is to live in peace and co-operation, war having become too self-destructive, it has become more urgent to develop a 'new man', one that is more sensitive and less aggressive. In practice such sensitivity means experiencing emotional vulnerability and that, in turn, means laying yourself open to experiencing (among many other things) fear and anxiety. Clearly those who believe such feelings are a sign of weakness or unmanliness require a major change of attitude.

This is not to say that aggression is bad and fear is good. On the contrary, some people have been so conditioned to think that aggression, protest and assertiveness are not acceptable that they are stuck with a disabling degree of anxiety against which they cannot fight. If it is true that for many years our society conditioned boys to think fear and anxiety were wrong, it is equally true that girls were taught that in many circumstances assertiveness was unacceptable. This is classically illustrated by the traditional roles of young men and women at dances. The girls waiting anxiously to be chosen could not counter their anxiety by taking action. They had to remain as 'wallflowers' or, if it went on for enough years, face the shame of being 'left on the shelf'. Of course they would have faced another kind of anxiety if they had taken the initiative but at least they could have been released from a very passive anxiety. The boys, on the other hand, had to be assertive in the face of their mates, often covering up their terror of being rejected by adopting aggressive, even loutish, behaviour.

To some extent society has changed its attitude to these things over the last twenty years or more. It is more acceptable for women to be assertive and for men to admit to being afraid, but it takes a long time for such change to take significant effect even without taking into account the individual's personal psychology and the particular burden of anxiety they may carry.

If you are able to think about your attitude to anxiety, not in a theoretical sense but as it applies to you as a man or woman, you may find that the first step in managing it better is simply (though it is not simple) to accept your anxiety as a God-given part of your humanity. Think of it, not as an enemy that is invading you, but as a friend, perhaps a child, hidden inside you, who is troubled and in need of understanding and support.

How do you, in fact, respond when someone tells you they are anxious or afraid? Because how you respond to other people gives a clear indication of the attitude you probably apply to yourself. I am assuming for the moment that such anxiety is related to a particular situation they have to face, say a child facing their first day at school or a friend having to speak in public. How do you respond when they say how anxious they are?

There are a number of fairly negative responses you might give. For example you might think that anxiety is rather shameful and embarrassing and try to ignore it as if the person had committed some awful social gaffe in expressing it. Or you might react in a rather judgemental way, especially if you are a Christian of a particular persuasion. You might tell them they ought not to feel anxious and that such fear shows a lack of faith or some other unacceptable spiritual weakness. Or again, you might feel totally unsympathetic and tell the unfortunate person to pull themselves together and 'be a man' (even if they are a child or a woman) as if that would in some way resolve the problem.

All these are very unsympathetic responses to the anxious person and of little help. On the other hand an excessively sympathetic response can also fail. Every time Tim felt anxious about something at school his mother would keep him away for the day. She felt anxiety was so unbearable in herself that whenever her son expressed it, even in a fairly mild way, she was overcome with a flood of sympathy and actively encouraged him to avoid what he was afraid of. Of course, he was never helped to find out what he could cope with and lagged further and further behind his friends at school as they grew in confidence.

93

Perhaps an overly sympathetic response like this is what you tend to give other people and have towards yourself.

A more helpful response, one that you might develop towards yourself and other people if you have a negative attitude, will, first, accept anxiety as a fact of normal life (unless it is out of all proportion to the situation), second, show understanding and compassion (especially when it is very distressing), third, help to look more objectively at what the options are and, fourth, encourage you or them to carry out what you have decided in the face of your fears.

The third of those things, looking at the options, can help you to feel an increased measure of control which can at once lessen the intensity of your anxiety. When you are faced with an anxiety-provoking situation you can develop tunnel vision about what you have to do so that you feel inescapably bound to what feels unbearable, as if you have no choice in the matter. It is this trapped feeling which can intensify the fear. One person I counselled, who suffered from intense feelings of anxiety and was trying to get back into employment, occasionally telephoned me in a near panic when he was due to go to work. He would say how anxious he felt, that he *had* to go to work and that he *couldn't*, he simply *couldn't*, go. I would simply remind him that he had a choice and stated the inescapable logic that if he really could not go then he could not go. Each time this happened, he would tell me later, he had immediately felt able to face his fears and go. Of course there may be times when we have no choice, but I think these occasions, especially in adult life, are much rarer than we usually suppose. We may not have the choice we most want, but that is a different matter. We may think that some disaster will follow if we change our minds. Disaster is highly unlikely. Though inconvenience or disappointment may follow, we usually still have a choice, and realising that choice can be important, not in cancelling out our anxiety, but in giving us a sense of greater control.

My emphasising the matter of choice is not to encourage people simply to back off and avoid anxious situations. On the contrary, as I have already tried to make clear, persistent avoidance of the situations which make us anxious tends to reinforce our fear in the long run. So you have sometimes to make a choice about whether an object of fear or a situation of anxiety is worth working at or whether you want to accept the limitation your anxiety imposes. For example you may feel very anxious about flying but accept the limitation on your freedom rather than fly and feel distressed. If you decide the limitation is not acceptable then you have to face your pain in some way or another. If you cannot manage it on your own, you may look for some professional help. Either way will involve some degree of distress.

Like all ingrained prejudices, your attitude to anxiety is difficult to change but it is possible to modify it in yourself at an intellectual level and even to begin to feel differently about it as you progress.

Sharing It

Just as the roots of our most basic anxiety are buried in our earliest experiences, and just as our relationships are among the most important of those experiences, so our present day relationships are very important in coping with our adult anxiety.

If you are someone who has typically hidden your anxiety from other people because of shame or the fear of being rejected as weak or bad, it can be a tremendous help to be able to share your feelings with someone else. I spoke about this when I was talking about the church and how it is often able to provide the kind of supportive fellowship where openness and trust are possible. But even if this is not available to you, happily there are many other people and situations where you can find someone understanding to talk to. You want someone who is comfortable with themselves without an overpowering self-confidence, someone who can listen without dashing to give advice or judgement, someone who can see the wood for the trees and someone who can respect your confidences without becoming over-anxious themselves or, of course, gossiping. I am not talking here about trained counsellors (though they should have all these qualities as a starting point to further skills) but people who may be friends, relatives or other professionals. Many priests, doctors, nurses and social workers are very experienced in listening to the anxieties of other people and are enormously helpful. However, it would be a mistake to assume that because someone is in a caring profession they will necessarily give the kind of response you need. Much of their work may require fast and very active intervention or be very technical and practical, and their skills are not likely to be helpful to you in your emotional distress.

You need a relationship you can trust and it is well to remember that trust is not something which comes in an instant: it needs time to develop. Especially if, in the past, your trust has been abused and your anxiety stems partly from that abuse of trust, it may take you a long time to risk saying very much. However, if you find someone who is reliable and understanding in small things you may be able to be more and more open about some of your deeper anxieties and find that simply sharing them is a great help. Do not expect your friendly listener to be a counsellor or psychotherapist to you, but if you find yourself beginning to uncover things which are specially disturbing and you feel yourself getting out of your depth, it may be wise to look for the more professional help I will talk about in the final chapter.

You may not be the sort of person I have just had in mind, one who has always hidden anxious thoughts and feelings. If, though, you are someone who has always had to tell someone else about it, you will doubtless have feelings rather different from those I have just described. Here I am not talking about an easy ability to share your anxieties and fears with someone close to you, but a rather compulsive need to pour them out on whoever is at hand. I realise that the compulsive need to do this can feel overwhelming, but it is very much to your benefit if you can develop the ability to contain yourself to some degree. The problem is that although people may be sympathetic at first, they soon become exhausted and may deal with it by pushing you away completely. This will only reinforce your sense of rejection and your fear of being abandoned by people and so increase your anxiety further.

Trudy, a young single woman, suffered a generally high level of anxiety and loneliness. Although she seemed to make friends very easily with her lively personality, the relationships never seemed to last. She felt people pushed her away after a time and she felt betrayed. Typical was her experience at her new church. On the first Sunday she was greeted by Helen at the end of the service. She felt an immediate attraction to Helen and talked at length, pouring out her hunger for love and how her last church had failed her. Full of sympathy, Helen invited her back to lunch, so that Trudy was able to share more and more of her hurts and anxious longings. She finally left in the early evening with an open invitation to call any time. Helen felt glad she had been able to help, though vaguely disappointed that all the talk had centred on Trudy.

Over the following two months Trudy came three or four times a week; she telephoned at some stage every day, always urgent, always anxious to talk. She said and felt that Helen was the only person she had in the world who would really give her time. Underneath she felt a restless anxiety that at any moment her time would run out and it would all come to an end as it always had. And of course, it did. First Helen's husband and children began to complain, then Helen herself felt more and more drained. She dreaded the phone ringing; she made excuses to get away; she had a migraine; but she could not bring herself to talk directly to Trudy about what was happening. Trudy, sensing Helen's increasing avoidance of her, became more anxious and increased her demands further until finally Helen and her husband attacked her about her demanding behaviour, telling her she was selfish and that she was no longer welcome to call. Trudy was deeply hurt about this rejection, felt quite suicidal and urgently needed to tell someone about it. That night she arrived on the doorstep of another person in the congregation to unburden herself.

Trudy's behaviour might seem a bit extreme (though it is not so uncommon as all that). She did eventually seek counselling and was greatly helped by the counsellor setting clear and firm time boundaries for their weekly sessions. She tried every way she could to make the counsellor give extra sessions or run over time, but to no avail. Gradually, as she was able to express her anxiety and have it contained within the counselling relationship, she was able to contain it more firmly inside her own mind without the compulsive need to pour it out. Eventually, she was able to make relationships in which she could talk about the things that mattered to her but set realistic limits to her expectations of other people. She found the ability to wait. She discovered that if she hung on desperately to people they would go, but that if she let them go, they would return.

If you recognise in yourself that tendency to pour out your anxieties rather indiscriminately on the people around you, see if you can set yourself some limits. If there is someone you are currently talking to about your worries in what may be an over-demanding way, discuss it with them and ask for their help in limiting the time or frequency of your talks. Bear in mind what I said before, that it can be helpful to think of your anxiety as a child inside which needs your help. Be understanding: do not be too strict and, on the other hand, do not let the child run out of control.

Some people find that their relationship with God, which they are able to focus in individual prayer, is another important way of containing their anxiety. But for many people such prayer, even spoken aloud, is too insubstantial; they need something much more solid to combat their restlessness. If this cannot be provided by the physical presence of someone else, there are a number of things they might find useful to contain and give some expression to their anxiety.

Containing and Shaping Anxiety

We described earlier how the physical body is affected by anxiety. Conversely, by attending to your physical state, you can positively affect your feelings. The things to focus on are muscular tension and the way of breathing, as these are especially affected by anxiety and can cause the symptoms to intensify. One method is to use some form of relaxation exercise, the other, oddly enough the very opposite, is to engage in vigorous activity. One helps you to let go of the tension in your body and regain control of your breathing, the other works through the tension, using the energy locked up in your muscles and exhausting you. Under these circumstances your breathing will tend to return to a more natural rhythm. Of course, as vigorous physical exercise should be followed by rest, it is arguable that both paths lead to the same goal.

If you decide to explore the use of relaxation techniques and want to learn more about them, there are books and audio-tapes available, as well as courses which teach relaxation. If your problems with anxiety are particularly difficult, you could ask your doctor if he or she is able to refer you to a clinical psychologist who will be able to teach you relaxation and help you to practise it.

One simple technique is to lie down and close your eyes in a place where you will not be disturbed; first focus your attention on your breathing by placing your hands on your midriff so that you feel it rising as you breathe in and falling as you breathe out. Do not breathe too rapidly or too deeply; make it slow and steady and easy. The exercise then continues by focusing on particular parts of the body, deliberately tensing and relaxing the muscles in harmony with your breathing; tensing as you inhale and relaxing as you exhale. You might begin with one extremity, say your toes, and slowly and systematically work through your body, tensing and relaxing, paying attention to small details and going back over parts which remain tense. Do not make hard work of it and become anxious about doing it perfectly: that will only defeat the whole object. When you have completed this physical exercise, you need something to hold the attention of your mind. Some people find they can focus on the physical rhythm of their breathing, others use a suitable piece of music, others, again, use fantasy, producing in their mind's eye a place and circumstances where they feel safe and at peace.

A technique such as this may be of considerable help, especially if you practise it regularly, but you may find it too bothersome and difficult. Occasionally people find that doing relaxation exercises on their own can have the reverse of the desired effect. As they release their normal state of tension, they experience a rush of anxiety or even a sense of panic. If you experience such a reaction, again, it would be well to seek some professional help.

Simply taking a long, warm bath or listening to an appropriate piece of music may be, for you, a more helpful means of relaxation. Remember that the essence of any exercise is to give yourself time, to relax your body and to slow down to let yourself be. There is a tendency when we feel attacked by anxiety to go faster as if to get away from the danger. We become like drivers suffering 'motorway madness' who accelerate to ever more dangerous speeds to escape the disorientating anxiety caused by thick fog. You need, rather, to recognise the feelings of anxiety and, deliberately, to slow down, containing the anxiety, then taking steps, as in relaxation, to establish some control.

Approaching anxiety through the mind or thinking processes is another useful way of containing and expressing it. Under the pressure of anxiety your thoughts can be chaotic, rushing round and round in your head in a fast and disorganised state. You need to get a handle on them, as with the body, to slow down and establish more control in order to shape and express your thoughts in a helpful way. The most obvious way of doing this is by writing, though drawing, painting, modelling or any other way of giving an external form to your anxiety might work for you. Your writing might be a straightforward description of your feelings or take some other form, like a letter to someone or an imagined dialogue that you would like to have. In such writing, which is only for your eyes, you can often express feelings which you would not allow yourself to voice to the person concerned but which you need to hear yourself say. It is important, if you write in this way, or draw, etc., that you then re-examine what you have produced and reflect on what you have said. Try to look at it with a little detachment, as something expressing the feelings and concerns of that anxious friend or child within yourself. You might then write something in response to strengthen your more realistic view of the situation.

Putting it down on paper as a means of shaping and expressing what is in your troubled mind is a useful tool in praying. If you experience the difficulty I mentioned earlier, that when your mind is in an anxious turmoil, thought or spoken prayer is too intangible, you may find that writing a letter to God, in which you can say exactly what you think, is more practical. If you think the idea sounds too trivial or childish, think again. It could be precisely that the anxious child within you needs a chance to speak out.

Some people make a regular discipline of writing about their life each day by keeping a journal. In this sort of journal, the focus is less on the external events that have made up the day and more on the feelings and reactions that have been experienced. Anxiety, anger, sadness and other emotional responses, are not avoided or denied, but both expressed and contained. This reduces any tendency to build up a large emotional backlog which threatens to burst out in an uncontrolled way, a cause of further anxiety.

One frequent feature of anxiety is that our chaotic thinking, as well as getting faster, begins to escalate into imagining more and more disastrous outcomes. Your child is five minutes late coming home and you begin to feel worried but think she has been held up; after seven minutes you are very anxious and feel sure she has had a serious accident; soon, in your mind, she is maimed for life. Within ten minutes you are convinced she has been kidnapped and is held somewhere and is suffering the same state of terror and near panic which you yourself have reached. You will never see her again. Or indigestion escalates into fatal cancer, an interview with the boss into summary dismissal and financial ruin, and so forth. Of course, people do suffer accidents and cancer and financial ruin but for the overly anxious person, these catastrophes rush into the mind with very little encouragement.

Similarly, fairly trivial incidents which may occur are felt to be potential disasters. Someone says, 'If I forget my lines in the play I will want to die.' 'If someone laughs I can't bear it.' 'I got angry and shouted at them at work. Now everybody will hate me.' Statements like these may be just colourful exaggeration, mere hyperbole, but they frequently betray a terrible underlying anxiety that the person's well-being is so fragile that it will not survive even a small mishap. These ideas, unchecked, cause anxiety to rise even further so, if you recognise this tendency in yourself or if you see it reflected in the kind of writing exercise I have suggested, you could well challenge it in yourself and counter it with more rational ideas.

I am not, of course, suggesting that such a rational approach to these anxieties will, by itself, deal with the underlying cause. I am concerned here with the need you may have to contain or manage anxiety which may run out of hand. As I have said before, if your anxiety is particularly troublesome and deep-rooted you may well wish to seek out more professional help which will enable you to explore it in an altogether more searching way.

9
PROFESSIONAL TREATMENT FOR ANXIETY

If you are suffering anxiety and decide you want to get further help there are a number of possibilities open to you. Although it must be said, in practice, what is accessible will depend on things like the services available in the area where you live, what treatment is offered by the NHS, what your GP's attitude is, whether there are voluntary agencies you can use or whether you can afford to pay fees if you need to go private. However, setting that aside for the moment, there are a number of treatments for anxiety, as there are for other emotional problems. In fact, there is a wider range than I can do justice to in this book. (I will use the word 'treatment' though that does not necessarily mean 'medical treatment'.) In what follows I will describe four approaches to treatment and to comment on each one. I will also mention some other issues that you might need to consider if you are thinking of looking for help.

I described in the first and second chapters how anxiety shows itself in physical sensations, in psychic symptoms (of the mind) and in disturbed behaviour. In the third and fourth chapters I talked about the importance of relationships in establishing and maintaining the roots of anxiety. When we come to look at the treatments for anxiety, you will see that different approaches put their main emphasis on one or more of those areas: some on the physical body, others on how we think about things, others on our emotions, others on behaviour, yet others on our early experiences and all our most important relationships. There can be fierce arguments among the different schools of thought about which approaches are most effective in helping their clients. Although I would certainly not go as far as to say that I believe they are all equally effective, I would make the point that any thoroughgoing treatment will affect all the areas of life I mentioned. I also believe, and this is well supported by some evidence, that the relationship between the counsellor or therapist and the client is a very important factor in any successful treatment.

Your General Practitioner

Your first attempt to get help for anxiety problems may be to go to your GP. You may get an appointment because you recognise that you are unusually anxious for some reason, or you may present a physical symptom which your doctor, perhaps to your considerable surprise, tells you is anxiety. The response you get from then on will depend very much on the personality of your doctor, what attitude they have towards emotional problems and what they believe, professionally, is the most effective kind of treatment for anxiety and other emotional problems. It will also depend on their previous experience of you as a patient.

Some doctors will give you time there and then for a brief talk to see if your anxiety is obviously related to some recent event or concern that they can respond to with advice, information or reassurance straight away. Others, because they work under such pressure of time, may offer you a longer consultation, as soon as possible, for the same purpose, though they will almost certainly not have the length of time available that a counsellor or psychotherapist can offer you.

If they feel the anxiety is related to a recent or obvious event which you are trying to work through, then as well as any advice or reassurance they give, they may try to relieve the pressure on you by suggesting a period off work or by prescribing drugs to help you sleep and/or ease some of the distressing symptoms. Of course, doctors vary considerably in their readiness to prescribe such drugs, just as patients vary in their willingness to take them. However, the symptoms of anxiety can be so desperate, urgent and demanding that the pressure to do something, and to do something right now, can be almost irresistible and drugs may offer the best immediate response. Indeed, they may be very useful in providing a short-term bridge over the chasm of fear whilst you work things out in other ways. What has been worrying in recent years is that large numbers of people have become dependent on drugs, used over long periods for treating anxiety and other emotional problems, and these drugs and their inevitable side-effects have created worse problems than they began with. Coming off the drugs has proved traumatic for some people, producing symptoms of intense anxiety and actual panic.

If the doctor prescribes drugs for your anxiety, do not be afraid to discuss the likely effects of these in the short term and ask about the longer-term effect if your anxiety continues to be distressing. It may be that your doctor will be able to refer you to a counsellor or clinical psychologist to work with you on the problem. It is open to you, if you choose, to refer yourself directly to a private counsellor or a counselling organisation. If you want further help within the NHS, you will, of course, need to go through your GP.

Counselling and Psychotherapy

These both describe talking treatments where the client or patient has a series of meetings with their counsellor or therapist to try to get to the bottom of their anxieties, to uncover the roots of their emotional problems and to come to terms with them in some way. Under this general heading I include treatments that may be described as: person-centred, psycho-dynamic, analytic, and so forth. They have many differences of style and theory but share fundamental ideas in believing that the roots of such disturbances as anxiety lie hidden in the mind of the sufferer and that they can be resolved in a particular kind of relationship. Whether this is called counselling or psychotherapy depends on a number of factors which professionals are always discussing but which need not concern the person looking for help. What must concern the person looking for help is that whoever they see is competent and properly trained. (For the time being I will use the word 'counsellor'.)

The counsellor will be there to listen carefully to what you have to say about your life and concerns and to respond in ways which will help you to open up more fully and to explore your underlying feelings. The counsellor will not direct what you should talk about but will nudge you in certain directions by the very way in which he or she responds to what you say. They may be less interested in what you think about things and rather more interested in what you feel. They may be less interested in the exact nature of your anxiety symptoms, but rather more interested in the emotional aspects of your present life and important relationships and (especially with some counsellors who are described as psychodynamic), with your childhood experiences and the relationship you had with your parents and other close family. They will see the symptoms as the tip of an iceberg, the whole of which needs to be attended to. When the underlying problems are worked through, the symptoms should lessen or disappear.

Such counselling seeks to unearth what has been hidden away as too dangerous or unacceptable, and to make it safe for that thing to be faced. In practice this means that the counselling is often distressing for the client as they accept into their minds thoughts, feelings and memories they have blocked. In this situation you may want to call it off if you become too anxious, and you will need confidence in your counsellor to see it through. This means that the counselling needs to help contain you in a safe relationship and, at the same time, enable you to express in words, or images, or tears, or trembling , what has been dammed up. Partly this safety is provided by your relationship with the counsellor but also by the practical arrangements for the treatment. You should expect regular sessions, normally at least once a week, and for the sessions to begin and end at the times arranged. You should expect not to be interrupted by callers or telephones during your sessions and for proper confidentiality.

It is also best, if you are wanting to have regular counselling such as I am describing, that you do not see someone who is too involved with you in other ways. For example, if you are a church-goer and someone in the congregation is a professional counsellor it is advisable not to go to them for sessions as you will almost certainly find that unhelpful: tangled threads can develop between you which may harm both your counselling and your friendship. Similarly, to see a counsellor who is already treating someone you are intimately related to is unhelpful and should best be avoided. By all means ask if they will refer you to someone else but try to avoid these conflicting roles.

Counselling and psychotherapy may be short or long-term, though even short-term may seem long to you if you are unfamiliar with its ways. Short-term could be up to twenty weeks, long-term will be open-ended and may extend into several years of regular sessions. In such cases what is being aimed at is not simply to do away with a difficult anxiety symptom but to bring about change in someone whose personality is deeply affected by how they have grown up and what has happened to them. In many cases the choice of short or long-term may depend more on availability and finance than anything else.

Counselling is available in the following ways:

1. A growing number of NHS general practices have a counsellor on the staff to whom the doctor can make a direct referral. This will tend to be short-term but should not be undervalued for that. In some cases it may lead to referral to a further agency.

2. NHS hospitals have departments of psychiatry, some of which provide this kind of psychotherapy. Again it may be limited in length, perhaps to three, six or twelve months, during which a great deal can be achieved.

3. Various voluntary agencies provide counselling. Although some are for particular problem areas, like marriage or drug abuse, others offer general counselling for emotional and relational problems and anxiety is high on the list of their experience. They will take referrals from doctors, social workers, clergy, etc. or directly from the client. Agencies of this kind often run on a financial shoe-string and clients are asked to pay a fee according to their means.

4. Many counsellors and therapists are in private practice. Like the voluntary agencies they accept referrals or can be contacted directly. Generally they charge fees they have set for themselves but some will negotiate with individual clients and take into account the financial means of the individual. Fees vary enormously and, at the time of writing, range between £20 and £40 a session with some practitioners falling off each end of that scale.

Cognitive and Behavioural Therapy

I am writing about these two forms of therapy together as they are often used together in practice. Cognitive therapy is concerned with the way in which you think about things and your ideas of the world and, indeed, your ideas about yourself. These are ideas you have developed or been taught by other people over the years as you grew up. By questioning and reassessing these ideas, you are faced with their frequently irrational and prejudiced nature. You are encouraged to challenge the irrational ideas and the fears they instil in you and so free yourself from their destructive power. You will recognise that there is more than a little basic cognitive therapy in the kind of response you get from people who are trying to help you in a common-sense way.

The parent who is trying to help their child face the anxiety of starting school may challenge their fear that they will not survive by pointing out the fact that all the other children are doing it successfully. This will help them contain their anxiety until they have the actual experience of coping with this new world. Then again challenges to our irrational fears may have very little effect on us other than to make us irritated with the would-be helper. For example, someone will point out that the spider you are terrified of cannot actually do you any harm, or that statistically your chances of dying in an air crash are lower than the chance of death on the roads, or that your fear that you are too fat is ill-founded given that you wear a size 8. By themselves these reassurances do little to help us free ourselves of what we already know is an irrational fear.

The cognitive therapist goes further and is skilled at getting the client to recognise whole patterns of irrational thought and particularly how one idea builds upon another, so creating the catastrophic thinking I referred to in the last chapter. Part of the aim is to recognise this process early on and to interrupt the disastrous line of thought before it builds upon itself. It aims to help the client develop a more realistic attitude to him or herself and to the world so that anxious thoughts do not run amok and drive them into self-destructive behaviour.

Generally speaking this cognitive approach is not enough, by itself, to treat anxiety fully, so the therapist uses behavioural practices to let the client gain further control. Control is a key word in all this as the therapist wants to help the client who feels that his or her life is controlled by anxiety to reverse this pattern so that they themselves are back in control. This means the client gaining greater control of physical sensations and actions as well as thoughts. Techniques include teaching the client physical and mental relaxation exercises, the control of breathing and the development of programmes of behaviour to help the client face up to and master situations which have previously caused them so much anxiety that they have run away.

As the client gains greater control and is successful in coping with anxiety, distressing symptoms grow less intense and may disappear completely in some situations, though it is important to remember, as I have said before, that some degree of anxiety is normal and healthy so that a complete 'cure' for anxiety is not on the agenda.

The relationship between the cognitive/behavioural therapist and the client is important as it is in all these situations. Each needs to respect the other so they can work in a co-operative way towards solving the problem. Unlike the counsellor/psychotherapist I described before, this therapist is not so interested in the psychological roots of your anxiety or whether it might have some symbolic meaning for you which can be uncovered and explored. He or she is more interested in the symptom itself; not in what has happened to you in the past but in what you are doing in the present.

Michael was referred by his GP to a psychologist who practised cognitive/behavioural therapy. Michael suffered from frequent attacks of anxiety which sometimes became so bad that he panicked and ran away. Over several years he had avoided more and more of those things which caused bad attacks. These included situations which took him away from home overnight and various others in which he felt trapped so that he could not get out at once if he wanted to: lifts, trains, crowds, theatres, etc. His life had become so restricted that it was affecting his work and making him depressed. These attacks had begun during a period of considerable stress at work and following an incident when his wife had been involved in a car accident.

The psychologist spent the early sessions asking Michael about his life and particularly about the anxiety attacks and when and how these occurred. He asked him to fill in a form each time he had an attack, rating how badly each symptom was on a scale of 1 to 10. He explained how the symptoms could escalate into a panic attack by desperate over-breathing. Later he asked Michael to list all the situations he feared, rating them from the least bad to the very worst.

Even at this information-gathering stage, Michael began to feel less afraid of his anxiety. He was encouraged to look at it objectively as something almost apart from himself that he might have some control over, rather than its being something bigger and more powerful than himself which always controlled him.

The psychologist helped him to think about the disastrous ideas that went through his mind when he feared an attack, thoughts that he would not survive. He was told that running away from anxious situations served, in the long run, to reinforce the anxiety further. Every time he ran for his life, the anxiety gained greater power and control whilst he lost more of both.

As the sessions progressed, Michael was helped to develop breathing exercises; he then set about a programme of action to tackle one by one his list of panicky situations, setting himself goals to reach before moving forward at each stage. He was encouraged to expect not an absence of anxiety but the ability to tolerate and master it. As his anxiety began to lessen its grip life became significantly freer.

This treatment went a long way to break the stranglehold that anxiety and panic were having on Michael's life though it did not, of course, even attempt to tackle the psychological and spiritual issues around his fear of separation and death. He would need, if he wished, to approach these somewhere else, for example with a counsellor or psychotherapist.

Cognitive/behavioural therapy is most commonly available through the NHS by way of a GP referral. Just as counselling is becoming more available at some general practices, so clinical psychology is coming into some surgeries and being available closer to home. Alternatively, the GP may refer you to the department of psychiatry or psychology at a local hospital to see someone who works in this way. A third possibility is for you to see someone privately, though this may still require a referral from your GP and will, of course, involve you in sessional fees as for psychotherapy.

Prayer Counselling

Some people within the Christian church use the skills of counselling in conjunction with prayer and the quotation of Bible passages in what is sometimes called the healing of the memories. Some people refer to this as 'Christian counselling', a phrase which unfortunately seems to exclude the many professional and voluntary counsellors who are working in Christian agencies but who do not use such practices; indeed, they may consider them to be inappropriate.

Ben, whom I mentioned in the first chapter, said that he had been helped considerably with his anxiety attacks by some Christians involved in the healing of the memories. The first stage of this stretched over two or three years during which time a Christian minister, in many informal conversations, helped him to recognise the way in which his anxiety attacks, related to fear of separation from his wife, possibly had their roots in early and traumatic separation from his mother. Bringing to mind some of the memories associated with this was very painful but, to some extent, he kept the pain to himself. The second stage which overlapped with the first was to take some practical action, in itself quite simple but up till then avoided. This was to accept friends' invitations to visit during periods when he was on his own. He had previously suffered his anxiety-ridden loneliness in silence and in a somewhat fatalistic way, as part of his feeling of impending doom. The third stage in this process of healing had occurred at a Christian conference when, in the atmosphere of a special service, Ben had opened up about his feelings and had, uncharacteristically, wept profoundly. This had been followed by the leaders quoting some appropriate Bible passages and saying some prayers for Ben's well-being.

Ben said, 'Going to the meeting was not the healing thing. It had been going on for some time, relating things that had happened to things in the past. Going to the meeting was an admission that that was where my problems lay. The prayer and expounding of the Bible was the public sign of the process taking place.

'Healing the memories is an understanding of them, an admission of them and the admission they are painful and hurtful. It is bringing them out into the open and offering them to God, in religious terms, for healing.'

I asked Ben if he expected to feel no further anxiety related to these early memories. He said that he didn't expect they would disappear but,

'I had a feeling of inevitability. Now there is a greater possibility. I'm not expecting an instant cure.'

Two things impress me about Ben's account: one is his rejection of any notion of the quick and easy cure, the second is the extent to which he takes responsibility for himself in a way that echoes the behavioural approach. In my experience this is not always the case with those Christians who become involved in prayer counselling who frequently do expect an instant cure. Prayer becomes for them either a way of avoiding an unpalatable truth or a way of putting an emotional sticking-plaster on a wound that needs more costly attention. This can be to help the counsellor feel better about a distressing situation whilst offering no long-term solution to the anxious sufferer. Prayer can also be a way of taking the passive route by placing the responsibility on God and foreclosing on the person's opportunity to grow and mature.

Choosing a Counsellor

This is a difficult matter to give general advice on and it is likely that most professionals, like myself, prefer to refer clients only to other counsellors and therapists whom they know personally or whose reputation they know. Just as church members may be Methodists, Roman Catholics, Baptists, Church of England or whatever because of where they are and who they know rather than because of the deep arguments which occupy theologians, so people may attend one therapist or another, at least in the first instance, because of where they are and who they know rather than any great conviction about one treatment or another. That being said, if you are looking for a counsellor, there are a number of things you might consider and, in the appendix, some names and addresses to follow up.

'What type of help do I need?'
As I have suggested already, you might see your GP about problems with anxiety and the GP may have helped you through the situation without either of you feeling you need a referral to anyone else. However, if you wish to take matters further, what type of treatment do you need? I have briefly described counselling and psychotherapy, which includes many variations on the theme of emotional exploration, and I have described the cognitive and behavioural approach. But what is best?

Much depends on the kind of person you are and the sort of values and belief you hold already, whether you feel intuitively drawn towards one type of treatment or another. You may prefer the more rational and direct approach of cognitive/behavioural therapy, or the more feeling-based approach of much counselling and psychotherapy, but this preference itself will be influenced by unconscious forces.

More objectively, it seems that the cognitive/behavioural approach is particularly helpful in treating anxiety where the symptoms are sharply defined in acute anxiety and panic attacks and where the person's attacks are triggered by special situations like open or closed spaces, or by objects of one sort or another. The treatment will be focused on the symptom and aimed at eliminating or greatly reducing it.

If on the other hand your problems with anxiety are more spread throughout your whole personality and you are bothered by disturbed inner feelings, or if your anxiety disrupts your relationships with other people causing conflict, guilt and depression, a type of counselling or therapy which is described as psycho-dynamic, person-centred or analytic will be most appropriate. In some cases both behavioural and dynamic therapies can run side by side to the sufferer's great good.

'Who do I go to?'
If you are looking for help within the health service then the route starts with your GP. If, on the other hand, you want to get

112

help privately or through another agency, like a counselling service, you might well get a recommendation from a professional worker like your vicar or minister, a social worker or, again, your GP, all of whom should know the services in your area. Alternatively you might contact the British Association for Counselling, which is one of our main national organisations for promoting good professional standards in counselling. It publishes a directory which lists organisations and individuals engaged in this work.

Your concern must be to find someone who is trained and competent, who works according to a professional code of practice. You also need someone you can intuitively trust. This does not mean that you will necessarily feel comfortable with them – after all, the counselling situation itself can be quite disturbing – but you will need to feel something of their integrity and empathy with you quite early on. At the first session or two, the counsellor will be assessing you as to whether he or she feels you can work together and you will need to make a similar assessment of the counsellor. It is not unusual for counsellors to suggest a limited number of sessions for a more extended trial period if the sessions are then to become long-term and open ended.

'How long will it take?'
This question is entirely understandable and is often addressed to the counsellor. It is rather like the old question about the piece of string and needs to be related directly to the individual situation. If your counselling is planned to be short-term and focused then the answer will be clear-cut and the sessions will come to an end at the set time. If your counselling or therapy is open-ended then that question must have an open-ended reply though, in practice, between a particular client and counsellor there may be much to say on the subject. However, bear in mind that if you start on the path of long-term therapy it is demanding in emotional terms as well as in time and, usually, money. On the other hand the rewards in terms of the psychological and spiritual qualities of life and, in this particular context, in relation to anxiety, can be very satisfying.

113

CONCLUSION

I will conclude (at least begin to conclude) where I began, with the opening words to chapter 1, 'Anxiety is natural to human beings, part of life's rich variety and closely bound up with excitement, energy and creativity . . . in excess it can become a living hell'.

Particularly if you are a Christian, do not suppose that your life should be or will be free of anxiety, as some have been mistakenly led to believe. On the contrary the spiritual life involves facing up to reality in all its aspects, and that means, among other things, facing your anxiety. If the pathway to freedom involves knowing the truth, that must include the truth which has been hidden and distorted through anxiety. When what is frightening and unacceptable is finally revealed, it will be transformed into something else and begin to lose its terrifying power.

A memory comes to mind of me as a child waking up alone in my bedroom with the weak light of the early morning beginning to dilute the darkness. I looked across the room and, in sudden terror, saw the unmistakeable shape of a man stooped, lurking behind the door. I was transfixed by fear, hoping that he had not seen me, staring at the profile of his face as his features became clearer in the dim light. I longed to call out to my parents in their room across the landing but I did not dare make a sound that would draw his attention to me. That way lay certain death.

I do not know how long I lay there in this state of fear-induced paralysis but gradually the light improved and the total immobility of the intruder began to cause me to doubt his reality. I was still too afraid to call for help but eventually I risked reaching out, cautiously, to the window above the bed and, lifting the curtain to give more light, revealed, to my immense relief, not a dangerous intruder but my dressing-gown, on its hook, on the bedroom door.

Anxiety can be a powerful force which can cripple, limit, impoverish and paralyse, but particularly so when the object of anxiety is hidden or distorted in the dark and gloomy recesses of

114

our minds. As a counsellor, I work with people who are motivated by distress or the desire to grow as human beings. They come, often with admirable courage and persistence, to 'lift the curtain' to shed more light on aspects of their lives which have been hidden in the darkness and, thus, to find liberation from their fears.

Rarely, of course, are the dangerous intruders merely dressing-gowns hanging on the door but, to change the metaphor, the monsters and ogres of the unconscious, once faced, are at least reduced to their human size and shape and begin to assume their proper proportions.

Now a word of caution. Although your anxieties may need to be faced in the process of liberation and growth, you cannot merely rush in where angels fear to tread. The wise counsellor will reflect the words of Jesus recorded in John's Gospel, 'I have yet many things to say to you, but you cannot bear them yet' (John 16.12). People may need emergency help to bear and contain acute anxiety with the help of drugs and other means of coping, but the deeper exploration of the roots of anxiety, which may happen through counselling and psychotherapy, is not a quick and easy task. On the contrary it is a hard journey, and for some a long one, with many resistances to overcome on the way. The client would quite naturally like a quick solution and may think the counsellor could provide one if he or she was not so perverse. Indeed, the naïve counsellor may wish to provide a quick solution and, thus, be able to bathe in reflected power and glory. But, if the counsellor is wise, he or she will know this is an empty wish and that matters cannot be rushed. Profound change may well include experiences of deep, liberating emotion and moments of dramatic insight linked to traumatic events in the past, but these are usually part of a longer process towards healing and wholeness. The wise counsellor will echo Shakespeare's words in Othello:

> What wound did ever heal but by degrees,
> We work by wit and not by witchcraft.

Further Reading

David Barlow and Jerome Cerny, *Psychological Treatment of Panic* (Guildford Press 1988)

Malcolm France, *The Paradox of Guilt* (Hodder and Stoughton 1967)

Calvin Hall, *The Meaning of Dreams* (McGraw-Hill 1953)

Sarah Horsman, *Living with Stress* (Lutterworth Press 1989)

Frank Lake, *Clinical Theology* (abridged edition) (Darton, Longman and Todd 1986)

R.S. Lee, *Freud and Christianity* (Pelican 1948)

Ainslie Meares, *Relief without Drugs* (Fontana 1967)

Alice Miller, *Thou Shalt Not Be Aware* (Pluto Press 1984)

Helpful Addresses

The following list of national counselling agencies is in no sense comprehensive but is one means by which you can discover what counselling and psychotherapy is available in your area. The British Association for Counselling is particularly useful in this way. Also remember that your GP may be a valuable first line of referral and that you will need to go through your doctor if you want a referral to a clinical psychologist, counsellor or psychotherapist in the NHS.

British Association for Counselling, 1 Regent Place, Rugby, Warwickshire CV21 2PJ Tel. 0788 578 328
National umbrella organisation for counselling and psychotherapy. Accredits counsellors and publishes a directory of agencies and individual practitioners.

Counselling Information Scotland, Health Education Board for Scotland, Woodburn House, Canaan Lane, Edinburgh EH10 4SG Tel. 031 452 8989
For information about counselling services and training available in Scotland.

Confederation of Scottish Counselling Agencies (COSCA), 64 Murray Place, Stirling FK8 2BX Tel. 0786 75140

Westminster Pastoral Foundation (WPF), 23 Kensington Square, London W8 5HN Tel. 071 937 6956
London–based counselling agency but with affiliated centres nationally.

Society of Analytical Psychology, 1 Daleham Gardens, London NW3 5BY Tel. 071 435 7696
Nationwide membership of Jungian psychotherapists and analysts.

Guild of Psychotherapists, 19b Thornton Hill, London SW19 4HU Tel. 081 947 0730
Nationwide membership of psychotherapists of various schools.

Clinical Theology Association, St Mary's House, Church West-
    cote, Oxford OX7 6SF Tel. 0993 830209
    Network of mostly church-based counsellors.

Samaritans, 10 The Grove, Slough, SL1 1QP Tel 0753 532713
    Emergency telephone counselling and befriending service.
    Branch numbers are listed in local telephone directories.

Cruse Bereavement Care, 126 Sheen Road, Richmond, Surrey
    TW9 1UR Tel. 081 940 4818
    Counselling for bereaved people. Local branches throughout
    the UK.

Relate, Herbert Gray College, Little Church Street, Rugby CV21
    3AP Tel. 0788 573241
    Counselling for marital, partnership, sexual and other inter-
    personal problems. Branch numbers are listed in local tele-
    phone directories under Relate or Marriage Guidance.

Also published by

Tri∕ＮＧＩＥ

LIVING WITH ANGER
by Myra Chave-Jones

Takes a positive view of anger and how it can be used as an important part of our lives.

FREE TO FAIL
by Russ Parker

A Christian exploration of the problems many people have with facing up to failure and its place in the spiritual life.

SEVEN FOR A SECRET THAT'S NEVER BEEN TOLD
Healing the wounds of sexual abuse in childhood
by Tracy Hansen

A moving account of a survivor of child sexual abuse working through the trauma induced by the return of repressed memories.

UNWORLD PEOPLE
For anyone who has felt unwanted, unusable, unloved
by Joyce Landorf Heatherley

Shows the growth of hope and faith after rejection, based on the author's own experience.

HOW MANY TIMES CAN YOU SAY GOODBYE?
Living with bereavement
by Jenifer Pardoe

A down-to-earth look at grief, with many everyday stories to give practical insights into what can be done to understand and help in times of bereavement.

BELIEF BEYOND PAIN
by Jenny Francis
Foreword by Richard Bewes

A remarkable insight into one person's physical pain and its effect on her life, faith and relationships.

LOSING AND LIVING
Thoughts on every kind of grieving
by David M Owen

Considers a range of personal losses – from bereavement of family and friends in death to the loss of our own health, youth or job. It includes many apt and revealing quotations which speak directly of the experience of grief.